WHAT ARE THE SPIRITUAL GIFTS?

DISCOVER YOUR SPIRITUAL GIFTS AND HOW TO USE THEM

CHRISTIAN QUESTIONS
VOLUME 2

WHAT ARE THE SPIRITUAL GIFTS?

DISCOVER YOUR SPIRITUAL GIFTS AND HOW TO USE THEM

J. D. MYERS

RedeemingPress.com

WHAT ARE THE SPIRITUAL GIFTS?
Discover Your Spiritual Gifts and How to Use Them
© 2018 by J. D. Myers

Published by Redeeming Press
Dallas, OR 97338
RedeemingPress.com

978-1-939992-57-4 (Paperback)
978-1-939992-58-1 (Mobi)
978-1-939992-59-8 (ePub)

Learn more about J. D. Myers by visiting RedeemingGod.com

Cover Design by Taylor Myers
TaylorGraceGraphics.com

JOIN JEREMY MYERS AND LEARN MORE
Take Bible and theology courses by joining Jeremy at
RedeemingGod.com/join/

Receive updates about free books, discounted books,
and new books by joining Jeremy at
RedeemingGod.com/reader-group/

TAKE THE ONLINE COURSE
ABOUT SPIRITUAL GIFTS

There is an online course related to this book.
The audio lessons and downloads in the course
will help you learn more about your spiritual gifts
and might also serve as a good small group Bible study.
Learn more at RedeemingGod.com/Courses/

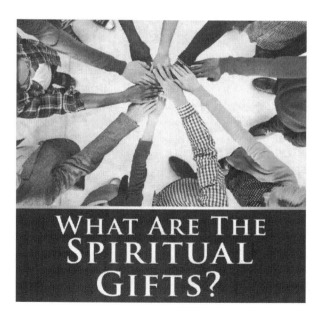

The course is normally $197, but you can
take it for free by joining the Discipleship Group at
RedeemingGod.com/join/

Other Books by Jeremy Myers

Nothing but the Blood of Jesus

The Atonement of God

The Re-Justification of God: A Study of Rom 9:10-24

Adventures in Fishing (for Men)

Christmas Redemption

Why You Have Not Committed the Unforgivable Sin

The Gospel According to Scripture (Forthcoming)

The Gospel Dictionary (Forthcoming)

Tough Texts on the Gospel (Forthcoming)

The Bible Mirror (Forthcoming)

The Grace Commentary on Jonah (Forthcoming)

Nin: A Novel (Forthcoming)

Studies on Genesis 1 (Forthcoming)

Studies on Genesis 2–4 (Forthcoming)

God's Blueprints for Church Growth (Forthcoming)

The Armor of God: Ephesians 6:10-20 (Forthcoming)

Books in the *Christian Questions* Series

Vol. 1: What is Prayer?

Vol. 2: What are the Spiritual Gifts?

Vol. 3: What is Faith? (Forthcoming)

Vol. 4: Am I Going to Hell? (Forthcoming)

Vol. 5: How Can I Study the Bible? (Forthcoming)

Vol. 6: Am I Truly Forgiven? (Forthcoming)

Books in the *Close Your Church for Good* Series

Preface: Skeleton Church

Vol. 1: The Death and Resurrection of the Church
Vol. 2: Put Service Back into the Church Service
Vol. 3: Dying to Religion and Empire
Vol. 4: Church is More than Bodies, Bucks, & Bricks
Vol. 5: Cruciform Pastoral Leadership (Forthcoming)

All books are available at your favorite bookstore.
Learn about each title at the end of this book.

TABLE OF CONTENTS

INTRODUCTION TO THE "CHRISTIAN QUESTIONS" BOOK SERIES

This "Christian Questions" book series provides practical down-to-earth answers to everyday Christian questions. The series is based on questions that people have asked me over the years through my website, podcast, and online discipleship group at RedeemingGod.com. Since thousands of people visit the site every single day, I get scores of questions emailed to me each month from readers around the world. Many of the questions tend to be around various "hot topic" issues like homosexuality, violence, and politics. Other questions, however, focus more on how to understand a particular Bible passage or theological issue. For example, I receive hundreds of questions a year about the unpardonable sin in Matthew 12.

I love receiving these questions, and I love doing my

best to answer them. But after I answered the same question five or ten times, I realized that it might be better if I had a ready-made and easily-accessible resource I could invite people to read.

So the goal of this "Christian Questions" book series is to answer the questions that people send in to me. At this time, I do not know how many books will be in the series.

Below is the current list of books in the "Christians Questions" series. Most of these are not yet published, but I include the list to show you where the series is headed.

What is prayer? *(Published)*
What are the spiritual gifts? *(Current Book)*
What is faith? *(January 15, 2019)*
Am I going to hell? *(Coming in 2019)*
How can I study the Bible? *(Coming in 2019)*
Why is the world so messed up?
Can God forgive my sin?
What is the unforgivable sin?
What is baptism?
What is the church?
What is repentance?
How can I evangelize?
Can I lose eternal life?
Why did Jesus have to die?
Should Christians keep the Sabbath?

What is demon possession?
How can I gain freedom from sin?
What is election and predestination?
Does God love me?
Why did God give the law?
Does God really want blood sacrifices?
What is sin?
What is the best bible translation?
Can I trust the Bible?

If you have a question about Scripture, theology, or Christian living that you would like answered, you may submit it through the contact form at RedeemingGod.com/about/ or join my online discipleship group at RedeemingGod.com/join/.

Some of these "Christian Questions" books are available as free PDF downloads to people who join my online discipleship group.

Visit RedeemingGod.com/join/ to learn more and join today.

CHAPTER 1

A PARABLE

Once upon a time, a CEO of a Fortune 500 company decided to send all of his managers an expensive gift for their loyalty and service over the years. He was an expert in working with people, so he carefully considered the strengths and abilities of each manager, while also taking into consideration their interests and hobbies. Then, based on what he knew about each person, he carefully researched and selected individual gifts for each manager. These gifts would not only delight and amaze them, but would also give them a sense of value, worth, purpose, and significance in life and at their job. Furthermore, each gift would also help them do their job with greater effectiveness and enjoyment. Each gift was perfect for each manager.

After the gifts arrived, the CEO had each one wrapped with beautiful paper and a large bow. Then he had the gifts hand delivered to each of his managers. Over the next several days, various managers started showing up in his office to thank him profusely for his gift. Many of them left notes of praise and adoration for his wonderful gift, and some even left a small gift themselves as a way of showing gratitude. The CEO also noticed over the next few weeks and months that many of the managers seemed happier and more content at work, and their output levels increased significantly. Their work became increasingly effective at helping the business accomplish its projects and achieve its goals.

Nevertheless, the CEO noticed that the work outcomes of four managers did not change significantly. Instead, their work production and quality actually decreased. This was troubling to the CEO, because he had spent so much time researching, planning, and purchasing these gifts for his managers. He began to wonder if he had made a mistake in getting the wrong gift for some managers, or if maybe they received the wrong gift. Since he deeply cared about each of his mangers, he decided to stroll down to the office of these four ineffective managers to see what the problem might be.

When he arrived in the office of the first manager, the CEO was shocked to discover that the gift had not been unwrapped. It sat on the manager's desk, glittering and beautiful with its wrapping paper and shiny bow.

"Why haven't you opened my gift and started using it?" the CEO asked.

The manager explained that the wrapping paper and bow were both so beautiful, and they matched the décor of her office so well, she thought it would be a shame to open the gift and ruin the paper, the bow, and how it brightened up her office. The CEO had a little chat with the manager, and encouraged her by saying that if she thought the paper and bow were beautiful, she would definitely love the gift inside, and it would be better than the package by itself. When she opened it, she discovered that the CEO was exactly right. Its appearance caused the paper and bow to pale in comparison, and it magnified the office decorations, and she immediately saw how it would also help her with her job.

Then the CEO went to the office of the second manager. Like the first manager, he was shocked to discover that the gift sat unopened on the desk. This manager was very business-oriented, and so the CEO had wrapped the gift in paper and a bow that was much more drab and business-oriented than the previous manager's gift. Therefore, he doubted that this manager cared much about the appearance of the gift, or how it matched the décor of his office (because there was none).

So he said, "Why haven't you opened my gift?"

The manager explained that he wanted to open it, and was planning on opening it soon, but he was so busy with all of his work, he had not yet found the time to open it. But after some encouragement, he opened the gift and discovered that it was the perfect gift to help him create more time in his job, and get more done in less time so that he could better enjoy his job and get home to spend more time with his family.

The CEO then walked down the hall to the office of the third manager. And while he expected to find the gift sitting on the desk still wrapped with its's box and bow intact, he instead discovered that this manager had indeed opened the gift, for it was sitting on his desk in all of its glory.

"I see you've opened my gift," the CEO said. "How do you like it and is it working?"

The manager sheepishly explained that while he loved the gift, and thought that it was the perfect gift for him, he hadn't yet started to use it because he wanted to read the manual first to make sure he was using it properly. The CEO encouraged him to start using the gift anyway, even before he had read the manual. He showed the manager that the gift was pretty intuitive, and didn't require many instructions. "You learn to use it simply by using it," he said. As he walked away, he saw the man pick up the gift and start to look it over.

The fourth manager was different than the other three. When the CEO walked into this man's office, he saw no sign or evidence of the gift at all. He didn't see a wrapped box on the man's desk, or the gift sitting anywhere in the office. So after a bit of small talk, the CEO inquired about the gift.

"How are you enjoying the gift?" he asked.

The man explained that while he was thankful for the gift, and saw how it might be helpful for his job, he thought his job performance was perfectly fine without the gift. So he had put it in the lower drawer of his desk.

The CEO invited the man to take it out of his drawer and try using it for a week or two. "If you still don't like using it after a few weeks, you can always put it back," he said. Then he left the office, knowing that the gift would never be put back into the lower drawer.

As you have probably figured out, this little parable is pure fiction. But it represents the way many Christians treat the gifts that God has given them, specifically, the spiritual gifts that they received from Jesus through the Holy Spirit when they became a new believer.

Some don't really even know they have the gift, and prefer to just look at the wrapping paper it came in, which is the enjoyment of Bible study and the church services they attend. Others know they have been given a gift by God, but they don't have time to figure out what it might be. They figure they are too busy with life and ministry to actually discover their spiritual gift. A third group has discovered what their gift is, but has not tried to use it. The gift looks scary because it invites them to step out in faith, or possibly make a fool of themselves in front of other people. Then there is the fourth group of people who feel they are doing just fine without their spiritual gift. They know what they are doing in life and ministry, and they are content with what they are doing, and feel that they don't need to put their spiritual gift to use.

To all these groups of people, God is saying "I gave you an amazing gift that is just for you. Nobody else has the unique gift which I planned, prepared, and freely provided just for you. Won't you discover what it is? Won't you learn how to use it? Won't you start putting it into practice? If you do, your life will change for the better. You will find greater significance, joy, and purpose in life. Your ministry will become more effective. Discover your gift and put it into practice. I promise you will not be disappointed."

Since you are a manager in God's business, what is your response?

The following chapters about spiritual gifts will help you unwrap your gift and start using it in your life. Let us begin by learning why God gave spiritual gifts.

CHAPTER 2

WHY DID GOD GIVE SPIRITUAL GIFTS?

Asking why God gave spiritual gifts to Christians is a bit like asking why God gave to you the various parts of your body. Why do you have a hand, a foot, or a mouth? The answer is that the various body parts are all necessary for the body to function the way God designed and intended it to function. So also with spiritual gifts and the church as the Body of Christ. God gave spiritual gifts to the church so that the church can function the way God designed and intended it to function.

Just as the various parts of our physical body allow us to live, exist, and function within this world, so also, our spiritual gifts allow the church to live, move, and have our being within this world. This church existence occurs in three general directions: toward one another, toward those in the world, and toward God Himself. We could also say that spiritual gifts have an inward, outward, and upward focus. Inward toward the church, outward toward the world, and upward toward God.

Let us look at all three directions.

EDIFICATION OF THE BODY

The first reason God gave spiritual gifts was so that each individual believer could work for the edification and encouragement of all other believers. God gave spiritual gifts so that we might help one another within the Body of Christ. This is the inward focus or direction. Paul points out in 1 Corinthians 12 that just as each part of the physical body is given for the benefit of the rest of the body, so also, each spiritual gift is given for the benefit of the rest of the church. If you have the gift of teaching, you should teach. If you have the gift of service, you should serve. All parts are necessary and important, and each part should fulfill its role for their own joy and that of others. Only in this way will the whole body remain healthy, live in unity, and grow into maturity.

EVANGELISM OF THE WORLD

But spiritual gifts are not only for the encouragement and edification of the body, but also for the evangelism of the world which leads to the expansion of the Kingdom of God on earth. This is the outward focus of spiritual gifts. One of the main reasons the church exists in the world is to show the world what it looks like when people follow God's instructions, and live like Jesus with love for others. Spiritual gifts of service and mercy, for example, are not only so that we might help and serve other members of the church, but so that we also love and serve those who are outside the church. As we live and love in this way, people are drawn to the church and into the full experience of the Kingdom of God.

This understanding of spiritual gifts as having an outward focus toward the world is critically important for the health and vitality of the church. Many believe that evangelism best occurs through big events, large group gatherings, splashy programs, and expensive mass evangelism campaigns. But God designed His church to work on a much smaller scale and in a more relational way. Evangelism works best when each individual Christian uses their spiritual gifts to love and serve the people God brings into their life. Truly effective evangelism is based on relationship building and interpersonal connections, and spiritual gifts are partly given for this purpose.

EXALTATION OF GOD

The final purpose for spiritual gifts is the exaltation of God. This is the upward direction of spiritual gifts. Some Christians seem to think that God is only exalted when they sing worship songs to Him in a Sunday service or offer praise to Him through prayer. While both of these do exalt the name of God, individual Christians primarily exalt God through how they live their day-to-day lives. And how we live our lives is guided by our spiritual gifts. As we use our spiritual gifts to teach, serve, love, and help others, God is exalted through our words and actions.

Furthermore, the diversity of spiritual gifts reflects the glorious creativity of God. As each person lives their lives in unique ways, God is glorified through the beauty of diversity. God is also glorified and exalted as each unique person works together with other unique people to achieve common goals. The diverse gifts working together in unity reveals the inter-relatedness of God. Since God is relational within the Trinity and within His connections to humans, the interaction of spiritual gifts in relational settings also reveals the nature and character of God.

CONCLUSION

So as Christians practice and implement their spiritual gifts, the church itself grows in strength and maturity, expands over the face of the earth into the lives of others, and brings honor and glory to God. Since these three tasks are the purpose and goal of the church itself, we can see that spiritual gifts are central to God's work through the church in this world. Without spiritual gifts, the church could not exist or function, nor could

God's work be done in the lives of others. It is critical, therefore, to discover your spiritual gift and start putting it into practice.

The first step in this process is to understand what spiritual gifts God has provided to the church. Only after you know what spiritual gifts are available can you begin to understand the spiritual gifts God has given you.

CHAPTER 3

WHAT ARE THE SPIRITUAL GIFTS?

There is some debate among Christians about how many spiritual gifts there are. Some people, for example, think that the Bible includes an exhaustive list of spiritual gifts, while others think that the gift lists are only a small sample of a much larger number of gifts, most of which are not mentioned in the Bible. Along with this, some people divide the gifts up into various categories, such as ministry gifts and miraculous gifts, or into three categories, such as teaching, service, and sign gifts. Furthermore, some argue that certain spiritual gifts are no longer in use.

This final question about whether certain gifts have ceased to exist or not will be addressed later. This chapter will address the questions of what the gifts are and how they can be categorized. Let us begin with discovering which spiritual gifts are mentioned in Scripture.

My belief is that the Bible does contain all the spiritual gifts. There are twenty-six of them. When people feel like they might have a spiritual gift that is not listed in Scripture, it is more likely that what they think of as a "spiritual gift" is instead a skill, hobby, talent, or ability. But these too work with spiritual gifts to help a person discover who God made them to be and what He wants them to do.

For example, some people are really good at math, but "Math" is not listed in Scripture as a spiritual gift. So a person who loves and enjoys math should seek to also discover their spiritual gifts so that they can partner their love of math with their spiritual gift as a way to discover the perfect ministry God has for them. In this way, while math is not a spiritual gift, it is part of their overall "SHAPE," as discussed in Chapter 8 of my book, *God's Blueprints for Church Growth*. Other talents and abilities are important considerations for the type of ministry you will perform, but these talents, interests, skills, and abilities are not spiritual gifts themselves, but work together with the spiritual gifts as listed in Scripture.

Before we consider the various spiritual gifts listed in Scripture, it is critical to first understand how and where the gifts are to be used.

THE USE OF THE SPIRITUAL GIFTS

Most books and teachings about spiritual gifts will correctly point out that spiritual gifts are given by God for the edification of the church. In other words, God gives spiritual gifts to Christians so that they can use these gifts to build up the church, the body of Christ. This is exactly what we learned in the previous chapter.

However, most of these other books and teachings think of "church" as the place that people go on Sunday morning to sit in a pew or a padded chair where they will sing songs, pray, and listen to a sermon. This mind-set about "church" causes people to then think that spiritual gifts need to be used within this setting. Spiritual gifts, therefore, are often explained as abilities or talents to help add more people to the Sunday morning church service, or help make disciples of the people who show up in the church building on Sunday morning.

Many pastors and church leaders will also hasten to add that spiritual gifts can also be used on days other than Sunday, but usually only at church-sponsored functions, programs, and activities. So pastors and church leaders will invite church members to not only use their spiritual gifts on Sunday morning, but also find ways to plug these gifts into the Tuesday night women's tea and Bible study, the Wednesday night children and youth programs, the Thursday night homeless outreach, or the Saturday morning men's prayer breakfast.

The church is none of these things. In fact, it is possible for all of these activities to take place without any involvement of the church. This is because the church is not a building, a place, or a set of programs. As I point out in my book, *Skeleton Church*, the church consists of the people of God who follow Jesus into the world.[1] The church is made up of people. People do not go to church; rather, the church goes with people. Wherever there are people who are seeking to follow Jesus, there is the church. This is true even if there is no building, pastor, budget, programs, doctrinal statement, prayer meetings, songs, or sermons.[2]

If Jesus leads a woman to stay at home so she can love and raise her children, she is functioning as the church, whether or not she and her children ever set foot in the "church" building down the street. If a man obeys Jesus in working hard at his job, loving his wife, and providing for his children, he is serving in the church, even if he never attends a "church" service, a Bible study, or a men's prayer breakfast.

Do you see? Since the church is the people of God who follow Jesus into the world, then whenever these people use their spiritual gifts in their day-to-day lives with the people God places before them, then these people *are* edifying and building up the church. They do not have to "go to church" to use their spiritual gifts, for they *are* the church, and can use their spiritual gifts wherever they are.

[1] Jeremy Myers, *Skeleton Church* (Dallas, OR: Redeeming Press, 2018).

[2] See my "Close Your Church for Good" series of books for a detailed explanation of why the church can more easily exist *without* all such things.

This is what the following book tries to point out regarding the use of spiritual gifts. Your spiritual gifts can be used anywhere at any time with anyone. And while "church" will be mentioned frequently in the pages that follow, do not make the mistake of thinking that "church" consists of the four brick walls and the white steeple on the corner of Main Street, or even the programs and activities that many Christians get involved in to purportedly "serve the church." Thinking this way about "church" will only lead to shame and guilt when you try to use your spiritual gifts.

Instead, recognize that you *are* the church, and you can use your spiritual gifts wherever you already are and in whatever you are already doing. If you ever start to feel guilty about how you are using (or not using) your spiritual gifts, "You're doing it wrong." Realizing what the church is (and is not) will help you gain the liberty, joy, satisfaction, and freedom that God intended you to experience in the use of your spiritual gifts. The spiritual gifts are not just for helping out at the building with the stained glass windows across town, but are to help you live and love like Jesus wherever you are, in whatever you are doing, with whoever is in front of you right now.

THE LIST OF SPIRITUAL GIFTS

Below is the list of spiritual gifts mentioned in Scripture. The brief list is then followed by an alphabetically arranged list, which includes an explanation of each gift.

Romans 12	1 Corinthians 12
Exhortation	Administration
Giving	Apostleship
Leadership	Discernment
Mercy	Faith
Prophecy	Healing
Service	Helping
Teaching	Knowledge
	Miracles
	Prophecy
	Teaching
	Tongues
	Interpretation
	Wisdom

Ephesians 4	Misc. Passages
Apostleship	Celibacy (1 Cor 7:7-8)
Evangelism	Hospitality (1 Pet 4:9-10)
Pastor-Teacher	Martyrdom (1 Cor 13:1-3)
Prophecy	Voluntary poverty (1 Cor 13:1-3)
	Craftsmanship (Exod 31:3-5)
	Creative communication (Acts 16:25; 1 Cor 14:26; Eph 5:19)

Administration: To steer a group toward the accomplishment of God-given goals and directives by planning, organizing and supervising others (1 Cor 12:28; cf. Acts 15:12-21). It is based on the Greek word, *kubernēsis*, which means "to steer, guide" and can be used in reference to the helmsman of a ship. Those with this gift understand the goals of the group, and the steps needed to achieve those goals. The group could consist of anything from a country or multi-national business to a local outreach ministry or a family. Politicians, CEOs, and mothers often have the gift of administration.

Apostleship (Missionary): To be sent forth to new frontiers with the gospel, providing leadership over church bodies and maintaining authority over spiritual matters pertaining to the church (Eph 4:11; 1 Cor 12:28; cf. 1 Cor 9:19-23; cf. Acts 12:1-5; 14:21-23). The word is based on the Greek word *apostolos,* which means "one sent forth." While the office of "Apostle" is no longer in use today, the gift of apostleship is still given by God in the form of missionaries who take the gospel to unreached people groups (See Chapter 7 in my book, *God's Blueprints for Church Growth*).

Craftsmanship: To make, construct, or build things (Exod 28:3-4; 31:3-5). Those with the gift of craftsmanship will often be skilled at using tools to help and inspire others through artistic, creative means. Those with this gift will also be good at making or fixing things, and will often find themselves drawn toward jobs such as architecture, engineering, construction, creative design, and culinary arts.

Creative Communication: To teach and share biblical and spiritual truths in creative ways that rely less on words and books and more on art, music, poetry, plays, photography, dance, and other similar outlets (Mark 14:26; Acts 16:25; 1 Cor 14:26; Eph 5:19). Nearly all artists, designers, actors, and musicians have the gift of creative communication. As people who capture God's creative beauty and wonder through the experience of the five senses, they use their gift to create beauty and inspire change in others.

Celibacy: To voluntarily remain single without regret and with the ability to maintain controlled sexual impulses so as to serve the Lord without distraction (1 Cor 7:7-8). Those with the gift of celibacy often devote their lives to a single cause, task, or mission, so that all of their time and energy can be devoted to this purpose, without the risk of neglecting a spouse and children. Just because someone is unmarried this does not mean they have the gift of celibacy. Those who desire to get married can and should do so. However, while looking and praying for the spouse that God has for them, they can use their time of singleness to focus on serving God and others.

Discernment: To clearly distinguish truth from error by judging whether a certain behavior or teaching has a divine, satanic, or human origin (1 Cor 12:10; cf. Acts 5:3-6; 16:16-18). Those with the gift of discernment also tend to be helpful in helping others know and understand their own spiritual giftedness. People with the gift of discernment often work as life coaches, counselors, and mentors.

Evangelism: To be a messenger of the good news of the gospel with their words, lives, and actions (Eph 4:11; cf. Acts 8:26-40). The Greek word, *euangelistēs*, means "preacher of the gospel" but since the gospel includes instructions for all of life and theology, the evangelist will not only preach the gospel, but will live out the truths of the gospel in a way that inspires others to do the same (See Chapter 7 in my book, *God's Blueprints for Church Growth*). Their life serves as a guiding light to others in this dark world. The evangelist is also proficient at discipleship, as they walk alongside others to help them practice the gospel in their lives. They will often live a transparent life, showing their failures and weaknesses to others, so that others can learn about God's grace, love, and forgiveness through them.

Exhortation (Encouragement): To come along side of

someone with words of encouragement, comfort, conso-
lation, and counsel to help them be all God wants them
to be (Rom 12:8; cf. Acts 11:23-24; 14:21-22). The
Greek word, *paraklēsis*, means "calling to one's side,"
and is related to the work of the Holy Spirit as our Para-
clete, our Comforter or Encourager (John 14:16, 26).
Just as there are people who serve with their hands,
these people serve and encourage with their words.
Those with the gift of encouragement include coaches
and teachers who see the potential in others, and cheer
them on to rise to this potential.

Faith: To be firmly persuaded of God's power and
promises to accomplish His will and purpose and to
display such a confidence in Him and His Word which
cannot be shaken by circumstances or obstacles (1 Cor
12:8-10; cf. Heb 11). Those with the gift of faith know
what they believe and why they believe it, and are able
to inspire action in others based on their beliefs. They
are often called upon to encourage others to step out in
faith and follow God to accomplish seemingly impossible tasks. Other people are drawn to those with the gift
of faith because they find hope and strength in their
presence. Those with the gift of faith often find themselves in positions of visionary leadership.

Giving: To share what material resources you have with
liberality and cheerfulness without thought of return

(Rom 12:8; cf. Acts 4:36-37; 2 Cor 8:1-5). They give without ulterior motive or conditions attached to how the money should be spent. Some believe that when God gives the gift of giving, He also gives the gift of making lots of money so that the giver can financially support multiple ministries and missionaries around the world. Givers often give away the vast majority of their substantial income, sometimes up to 90% or more. In ancient Roman society, those with the gift of giving would be called Patrons.

Healing: To be used as a means through which God makes people whole and restores health to the sick, whether they are physically, emotionally, mentally, or spiritually ill (1 Cor 12:9, 28, 30; cf. Luke 9:1-2; Jas 5:13-16). Note that healing is not just miraculous healing, but the ability to use modern medicine and science to bring about healing in someone's mind or body. As a result, those with the gift of healing often find themselves in the fields of medicine and psychology.

Helping: To render support or assistance to others so as to free them for other work (1 Cor 12:28; cf. Acts 6:2-4). They bear the burdens of others to help them accomplish their work more effectively. Those with the gift of helping find great satisfaction in doing menial jobs behind the scenes so that others can be freed up to do other tasks. While those with the gift of helping rarely receive much recognition or praise, the truth is that without their gifts, the people who often receive recognition and praise would not have the time or energy to do what they do. Therefore, the gift of helping actually allows the other more "flashy" gifts to function. People such as janitors, custodians, nurses, parents, classroom aids, assistant coaches, secretaries, and all other "behind the scenes" staff likely have the gift of helping.

Hospitality: To warmly welcome people, even strangers, into one's home as a means of serving people who need food or lodging (1 Pet 4:9-10; cf. Gen 18:1-15). They cheerfully open their homes to care for other people. True hospitality is not standing behind a counter at the "Hospitality Center" that exists in some church buildings, but requires you to open your own home to other people so they can share your food and enjoy a roof over their heads. The Greek word, *philoxenos*, means "love of strangers." Note that in biblical times, these "strangers" were usually Christians who were traveling from town to town and came with letters of introduction, but it does not have to limited to only Christians. Non-Christians can (and should) be welcomed into your home as well. However, wisdom dictates that you should know something about the people you invite into your home, for it is always unwise to welcome *complete* strangers into one's home.

Interpretation of Tongues: To translate the message of someone who has spoken in another language for those who do not understand what was said (1 Cor 12:10; 14:27-28). As will be discussed briefly below, the gift of tongues is speaking in an actual foreign language. Therefore, in order for what is said to make sense to other people, it must be interpreted. Those with the gift of interpretation are sometimes able to understand what foreigners are saying, even if they have never learned the other language. Some who have the gift of interpreting tongues also find that they can quickly and easily learn foreign languages.

Knowledge: To seek to learn as much about a particular subject as possible through the gathering of information and the analysis of that data (1 Cor 12:8; cf. Eph 3:14-19). Those with the gift of knowledge enjoy reading and studying, and find that they are able to easily learn, retain, and recall facts. Those with the gift of knowledge are also able to synthesize various streams of learning to develop new ideas and insightful ways of looking at difficult topics. People with the gift of knowledge find themselves in the fields of science, mathematics, literature, history, and theology.

Leadership: To live in front of people in such a way as to motivate others to change their lives, follow directions, influence decisions, and get involved in their community and the world so that all harmoniously work together to accomplish common goals (Rom 12:8; cf. Exod 18:13-16; Judg 3:10; Heb 13:7). Those with the gift of leadership inspire others to follow without feeling the need to command, threaten, or cajole. Those with the gift of leadership often become actual leaders in their communities, businesses, or countries.

Martyrdom: To give over one's life to death for the cause of Christ (1 Cor 13:3). Those who give their life in this way are called "martyrs," from the Greek word, *marturos,* meaning "witness." Giving one's life for Jesus is a great way to be a witness for Him. Nevertheless, while one can feel that they would be willing to die for Jesus Christ, it is not something which you can plan, prepare, or practice. Therefore, a person cannot know if they have the gift of martyrdom until they actually become a martyr. As a result, the Spiritual Gift inventory test at the end of this book does not contain any questions about martyrdom.

Mercy: To be sensitive toward those who are suffering, whether physically, mentally, or emotionally, so that you feel genuine empathy and compassion for others in their misery (Rom 12:8; cf. Luke 10:30-37). Those with the gift of mercy are able to empathize with those in pain, so that they speak words of compassion and offer acts of love to help alleviate others in their distress.

Those with the gift of mercy often devote large amounts of time to help others in need, and can typically be found in the positions as counselors, mentors, and service positions where they work with the sick, elderly, mentally ill, and handicapped.

Miracles: To be enabled by God to perform mighty deeds which witnesses acknowledge to be of supernatural origin and means (1 Cor 12:10, 28). Those with the gift of miracles cannot promise that God will work miracles in their life, or the life of someone else, but often see God work the impossible in response to their prayers and acts of faith. This gift often works in coordination with the gifts of faith and healing.

Pastor-Teacher: To be responsible for the spiritual care, protection, guidance, and provision of a group of believers entrusted to one's care (Eph 4:11; cf. 1 Pet 5:1-11). Since the word *pastor* is related to the word for *shepherd,* the pastor-teacher often uses preaching and teaching as a way to lead, guide, and protect others (See Chapter 7 in my book, *God's Blueprints for Church Growth*). Those with the gift of pastor-teacher tend to be more relational than the teacher, and are therefore better at providing overall care for the spiritual well-being of the church.

Prophecy: To speak forth the message of God to His people (Rom 12:6; 1 Cor 12:10; Eph 4:11; cf. Isaiah–

Malachi; 1 Cor 14:1-5, 30-40). The Greek word, *prophētēs,* refers to the forth-telling of the will and word of God. It does not primarily refer to foretelling the future, but to forth-telling God's will (See Chapter 7 in my book, *God's Blueprints for Church Growth*). One with the gift of prophecy will speak God's Word with boldness and clarity to call God's people to repent from sin and return to God's ways.

Service: To identify undone tasks in God's work, however menial, and use available resources to get the job done (Rom 12:7; cf. Gal 6:1-2). The Greek word, *diakonia,* means "servant, attendant," and refers to someone who runs errands for others. They take care of the day-to-day physical details for leaders and spiritual directors to free them up to take care of spiritual matters. Though this spiritual gift sounds lowly, it is one of the backbone gifts of any community or group. Without people to take care of these routine tasks, no business or organization would be able to properly function.

Teaching: To instruct others in a passionate, logical, succinct, and systematic way so as to communicate pertinent information for true understanding and personal growth in others (Rom 12:7; 1 Cor 12:28; cf. Heb 5:12-14). The gift of teaching differs from that of pastor-teacher in one main way: the pastor-teacher usually teaches with "pastoral" concerns in mind. The preaching and teaching of the pastor-teacher tends to be more practical, attempting to address the needs and concerns of the average Christian. The teacher, however, might be more academic and will often lack the interpersonal skills necessary to serve as a pastor-teacher. Most skilled teachers and professors have the gift of teaching.

Tongues: To speak in a language not previously learned so unbelievers can hear God's message in their own language (Acts 2:4; 1 Cor 12:10; 14:27-28). If those who are present do not understand what is said, tongues must always be interpreted. If there is no interpreter, the speaker must remain silent. There is no evidence anywhere in Scripture that the gift of tongues causes a person to speak in a secret prayer language. Speaking in tongues always involves speaking in another "tongue," or language. As such, it might be more precise to speak of people having the gift of *languages*, which helps them quickly learn foreign languages. (See the chapter on tongues later in this book.)

Voluntary Poverty: To purposely live in an impoverished lifestyle to serve and aid others with your material resources (1 Cor 13:3). Those with the gift of poverty love to give away their money and possessions so that they might live simply, generously, and sacrificially. They often view possessions and money as a hindrance to ministry, and use their money to meet the needs of those poorer than themselves. Voluntary poverty differs from the gift of giving in that those with the gift of giving might be rich, whereas those with the gift of voluntary poverty tend to live among the poor so that they might love, serve, and identify with them.

Wisdom: To apply knowledge to life in such a way as to make spiritual truths quite relevant and practical in proper decision-making and daily life situations (1 Cor 12:8; cf. Jas 3:13-17). Those with the gift of wisdom are often very good in counseling situations, and find that people often come to them for advice. They are very good at understanding God's will in various situations, and helping people understand the right decisions to make in life.

Related to the list of spiritual gifts, some try to categorize the gifts into various groupings. For example, many divide the gifts into two categories: ministry gifts and miraculous gifts. Yet are not miracles also a form of ministry? The gift of healing ministers to the physical body and the gift of tongues ministers to people who speak other languages. So this two-fold division is unsatisfactory, since all spiritual gifts are "ministry" gifts.

The same is true for the three-fold gift division of teaching gifts, service gifts, and sign gifts. While it is true that some gifts tend to use words (whether written or spoken) while other gifts focus on helping others with your hands, all uses of the gifts are still a form of service to others, and all the gifts serve as a sign to others that God is at work in our midst. A powerful sermon from Scripture that convicts hearts and calls people to follow Jesus is just as much a sign that the Holy Spirit is at work in our presence as is the gift of miracles or healing.

Furthermore, since most human learning is done through imitation of others and the vast majority of human communication is done through body language, one does not have to say a single word in order to teach and train others. By loving and serving others, you naturally teach them about the love of God and how they too can treat other people, even if you never say a single word to them about such subjects. Therefore, all gifts are sign gifts, and all gifts are service gifts, and all gifts are teaching gifts. Here too, the attempts to categorize and divide the gifts break down.

One reason that some people try to categorize the gifts is because they say that only some of the gifts are active today while others are no longer being used. This issue will be briefly addressed later, but for now, since we see that there is no good or logical way to categorize the gifts, this is one indication that all the gifts are likely still in use.

So rather than worrying about whether you have a ministry gift or a miraculous gift, the best approach is to simply figure out which gifts you have and then start using them for ministry. Thankfully, as we will learn in the next chapter, it is not too difficult to identify your spiritual gifts.

CHAPTER 4

HOW CAN I KNOW MY SPIRITUAL GIFT?

There are many ways to discover your spiritual gifts. I encourage you to use all of them as a way to identify and confirm your spiritual gifts. If you use just one method, there is a chance of improperly identifying your spiritual gifts, thereby leading to frustration in life and ministry. But if you start with one method of identification, and then use the other methods to confirm or change the results of the first method, you will often end up properly identifying your spiritual gifts.

SELF-ANALYSIS

The first (and preferred) method for identifying your spiritual gift is to look into your own heart and mind and consider which spiritual gifts you would like to have. Of course, when you do this, you are not just trusting your own heart and mind to "figure it out," but are actually looking for the still small voice of the Holy

Spirit to point out to you which gifts you have been given. As these gifts are *spiritual* gifts, we must first look to the Holy Spirit for leading in this matter.

Even if you are uncomfortable or unaware of how to listen to the voice and leading of the Spirit, it is still important to try. The Spirit is always whispering to you, and you will only learn to sense His leading and direction as you attempt to listen to what He is saying. Furthermore, once you discover your spiritual gift, it will be important to continue to rely on the leading of the Holy Spirit for how He wants you to use your spiritual gift. So you might as well begin by seeking His input on the identification of your gifts.

To do this, just return to the previous chapter where the spiritual gifts are listed and read through them slowly, trying to discern which ones might be true of you. As you read the descriptions, look for ones that might be interesting or that sound intriguing. Look for gifts that pull on you heart or that seem to describe your interests and desires. The gifts that you feel drawn to are possibly the gifts that God has given to you.

Remember, of course, that there is a difference between the gifts you *want* and the gifts you *have*. You can be wrong in your feelings and desires. So as you read through the spiritual gifts, not only think about the gifts you would like to have, but also the sorts of things you have actually done in life which have given you joy and satisfaction. For example, almost everybody wants the gift of giving since it is often accompanied by wealth. But if you have never been rich, and do not see that you are likely to become rich, and do not have a history of giving away large sums of money, then these are good indications that even though you desire the gift of giving, you likely do not have it. Pairing the gifts you desire with the sorts of activities and actions you have actually done provides the best self-analysis of the spiritual gifts you might have.

Once you have done this self-analysis, you can move on to the next four ways of identifying your spiritual gifts, as they help confirm which spiritual gifts you might have.

SEEK THE INPUT OF OTHERS

Since the gifts are given for the edification of others, one way you can gain insight into which gifts you might have is by seeking the input of others. This is especially effective when you seek the input of people who know you well, and who have seen you serve and interact with other people.

This method of discovering your spiritual gifts is especially effective if you can ask someone who has the spiritual gift of discernment. God has specifically enabled those with the gift of discernment to see, understand, and recognize the various spiritual gifts in other people. Of course, they don't do this through some sort of magical "fortune-telling" experience where their eyes roll back in their head and they read tea leaves in a cup. No, they discern these things by getting to know you and observing your life. So even here, if you are going to ask for the input of others, you must not ask strangers.

This shows why it is important to be involved in the lives of other people. It is only with other people that you can practice your spiritual gifts, and it is only with other people that you can ask for their input about your gifts. If you are not part of a gathering of believers, it may be difficult for you to discover your spiritual gifts, or for others to provide input on what your gifts might be.

Remember, of course, that the smallest, most basic gathering of believers is your immediate family. So as you seek the input of others about your spiritual gifts, start with your parents, children, spouse, and siblings. They know you best, and will be able to provide some of the most helpful input and advice about your spiritual gifts. Other than family, you can also ask your close friends and coworkers. It will not be of any benefit to ask people who rarely see you or interact with you on a daily or weekly basis.

SPIRITUAL VOID ANALYSIS

One of the very best ways to discover your spiritual gifts is to take note of your criticisms and complaints about church. When you look at the local church body you are part of (or the worldwide church as a whole), and see areas of weakness, fault, or neglect, you have just discovered what God wants you to be doing in the church. In other words, if there is something you think that everybody in the church should be doing (but aren't), then you have just discovered what it is *you* should be doing.

For example, if you think the church is doing a poor job of teaching Scripture to others, then this likely means that you have the spiritual gift of teaching, and you are supposed to start using it. If you think the church should be serving the poor in your community, this probably means you have the gifts of service, mercy, or hospitality. If you complain that the church is not creative and artistic enough in its music, programs, or decorations, this likely means that you have the gift of creative communication.

As you can see, this method of discovering your spiritual gifts is extremely helpful, for it not only allows you to accurately identify your spiritual gifts, but it also spurs you on to actually use your gifts to meet the need that you see, rather than just sit on the sideline (or in the pew) complaining about all the things the church should do differently. If you see a void in the church, it is likely because God wants you to fill it and has specially gifted you to do so.

SPIRITUAL GIFT ANALYSIS

You can, of course, always take a spiritual gift inventory test as a way of discovering your spiritual gifts. There is one such test at the end of this book (see Appendix 1). Many of these tests are somewhat like personality tests, where the person answers a series of questions and then scores the test based on their answers. The scores provide insight into which spiritual gifts the person might have.

However, it is necessary to state a warning about these sorts of tests. Of the five available ways for discovering your spiritual gifts, this method is the least reliable. This is simply due to the fact that test results are easily undermined by various outside factors. Not only is it possible for the questions to be misunderstood, but when a person takes the test, a whole host of outside factors can drastically alter the outcome of these sorts of tests, such as where they took it, how they are feeling at the time they took it, and what they just heard or read before they took it.

I once ran a little experiment where I decided to test a group of men by giving them the same exact test two weeks apart. During the first week, I taught a 30-minute lesson about the miracles of Jesus and the importance of faith for seeing miracles today. Then I gave the men the test, and had them turn it in to me for scoring. The next week, I told the men that I had somehow misplaced the tests, and I apologetically asked them to take it again. But this time, I preceded the test with a 30-minute lesson on the importance of Scripture memorization, Bible study, and reading good books about theology. Then they took the test a second time.

The (unsurprising) results of these two tests were that even though the same men took it only two weeks apart, the results from the first week showed that the majority of the men had spiritual gifts of miracles and faith, while the results from the second week showed that the majority of them had spiritual gifts of teaching and knowledge. The clear influencing factor which explains the difference was the lesson they had just heard me teach.

So it is fine to take spiritual gift inventories like the one at the end of this book, but you must recognize that these tests are easily skewed by how you are feeling, what you have been reading or hearing, and a wide variety of other factors. If you take a spiritual gift inventory test, it is best to take it multiple times over the span of a several months or years, and to use it in coordination with the other four ways of discovering your spiritual gifts. It is especially important to use the fifth and final way, discussed below.

SERVE AND EXPERIMENT

The last and most important way of discovering your

spiritual gifts is simply to use the spiritual gifts you think you have. There is no better way to discover and strengthen your spiritual gifts than by serving and experimenting with them in the context of a local body of believers. Regardless of what other method you might use for discovering your spiritual gifts, this is the one method you must not neglect.

The reason this method is so critical is because it will either confirm or contradict the initial identification of your spiritual gifts. When you find your spiritual gift and start putting it into practice, you will experience greater excitement and energy in the ways you interact with others, and find that they grow closer to Jesus as a result of your work with them. Furthermore, as you practice your gifts, you will get better and better at using them, and will begin to influence and edify more and more people.

The exact opposite happens, however, when you try to use gifts that you think you might have, but in fact do not. For example, if you think you have the spiritual gift of teaching, but people fall asleep when you teach, and few return to hear you teach, then this might be a good sign that teaching is not your gift. If you think you have the gift of mercy, but you get upset and angry at people who don't seem to take your advice and don't change fast enough to suit your expectations, then this might be a good sign that you don't have the gift of mercy.

So if you think you have certain spiritual gifts, but when you attempt to put them into practice, you get frustrated and angry while other people are not encouraged or edified, then this is a good sign that the spiritual gift you are trying to practice is not actually your spiritual gift. If you initially misdiagnose your spiritual gift, do not be discouraged, but simply go back and try to discover your spiritual gift again. It usually will not take more than two or three attempts before you find the spiritual gift God has given to you, and you begin to see Him work through your life to touch the lives of others.

One of the reasons that some people experience this initial misdiagnosis is because they have been taught that some spiritual gifts are better than others, and they want one of these "better" gifts. But is this true? The answer is "No," as we see in the next chapter.

CHAPTER 5

ARE SOME GIFTS BETTER THAN OTHERS?

Various groups of Christians seem to think that some spiritual gifts are better than others. For example, many charismatic and Pentecostal groups place a heavy emphasis on the gifts of tongues, miracles, and healing. They do this partly because these three gifts provide a good "show" to the people in the pew, but also because there are a few texts which seem to indicate the importance of these gifts. For example, Acts 2 shows that tongues came upon those who were in the Upper Room when they first received the Holy Spirit. Therefore, some teach that tongues is a sign that someone has received the Holy Spirit. Also, 1 Corinthians 14:22 says that tongues are a sign to unbelievers.

Related to this, miracles and healing are viewed as a way of verifying the truth of what someone is teaching. For example, when Jesus was challenged about the truth of His teachings, He pointed people to the signs He had performed as evidence of His authority and identity (cf.

Luke 7:18-22). The apostles also seemed to follow a similar practice in the Book of Acts as they carried the gospel message to other regions of the Roman Empire.

Then there is Paul's statement in 1 Corinthians 12:31 where he seems to instruct the Corinthian Christians to eagerly desire the greater gifts. Some believe that since Paul has just mentioned tongues and healings (1 Cor 12:30), it is these gifts that are "best" or "greater" and therefore, it is these that Christians should seek after and desire. Supporters of this view point out that Paul's words in 1 Corinthians 12:31 are better translated as "You are eagerly desiring the best gifts." Further support for this view is found in 1 Corinthians 14, where Paul goes into great detail about the use of tongues in the meeting of the church. Some have used this text to say that tongues is one of the better gifts. After all, the Corinthian Christians were emphasizing tongues and Paul seems to say that they are eagerly desiring the best gifts. Furthermore, Paul then goes on to provide careful instruction of the use of tongues. So does this mean that tongues truly is one of the better spiritual gifts?

Mostly likely not. Many believe that while Paul does indeed spend a lot of time writing about tongues, the overall tone of Paul's discussion is corrective. Yes, the Corinthians are emphasizing tongues, but the overall purpose of Paul's letter, and the immediate context of these chapters, is to correct various Corinthian abuses. Tongues is one of those. And while some of these scholars agree that 1 Corinthians 12:31 could be translated as suggested above, they say that Paul's tone is one of sarcasm or irony. If so, Paul should be understood as saying, "But you are eagerly desiring *what you think to be* better gifts, *but they really are not.* Let me show you a more excellent way." Then Paul goes on to write about love (1 Cor 13), and how intelligible words are more loving and edifying than unintelligible words (1 Cor 14:12-19).

So in this second view, Paul is criticizing the Corinthian Christians for their overemphasis upon tongues and is instead instructing them to seek better gifts, such as those that edify and instruct the entire church (1 Cor 12:12-26; 14:12-19). Paul states later that it is better to speak five intelligible words than ten thousand words that cannot be understood. This seems to show that gifts such as prophecy and teaching are more important to Paul than gifts of tongues and miracles.

However, I believe that this debate about which gifts are better misses the entire point of Paul's overall argument. Paul's point is that no gift is better than another. Though the Corinthian Christians did indeed seem to place a higher degree of emphasis and importance on various "miraculous" gifts, Paul tries to rein them in by pointing out that all the gifts are equally important. This truth is especially seen in 1 Corinthians 12:12-26, where Paul uses body imagery to show that there are no lesser or greater parts of the body, for all parts depend and rely upon all the other parts. While it is true that some parts "seem to be weaker" (1 Cor 12:22) or "less honorable" (1 Cor 12:23), it is these parts that tend to be more important or bestowed with greater honor (1 Cor 12:23-25). All parts are equally necessary, important, and honorable, and if one part is despised, rejected, or neglected, the entire body suffers (1 Cor 12:26).

The overall message of Paul, therefore, is that no gift is better than another, for all gifts are given by God. All the gifts are required for the proper functioning of believers as the Body of Christ to love and serve others in this world. Those gifts that have the appearance of being less important or less honorable, are actually those who are given additional importance and honor so that they are raised up to equality and value with all the other gifts.

The bottom line is this: Whatever gifts you have been given by God are critically important for your life as a follower of Jesus as you use them in this world. But this does not make your spiritual gift more important than the gifts of others. The spiritual gifts of others are just as essential and important as yours. When we fail to remember this, we fall prey to the dangers of spiritual gifts, which we learn about in the next chapter.

CHAPTER 6

THE DANGERS OF THE SPIRITUAL GIFTS

As wonderful as spiritual gifts are, they come with inherent dangers. While there are specific dangers for each gift, there are also two general dangers that all the gifts have in common. Let us first look at these two general dangers, and then we will briefly consider the specific dangers of each individual gift.

TWO GENERAL DANGERS

The first danger that all the spiritual gifts have in common is the tendency of many to only use their spiritual gifts for other Christians, or "in the church" on Sunday morning. Frequently, when people start to think about how they can use their spiritual gifts, they limit their ideas to only those ministries or people which will help their local church body.

For example, evangelists might focus primarily on getting people to "come to church." Those with hospitality might only invite "church members" over for dinner. People who love to serve might only look for opportunities to help in the church functions and programs.

This is a danger because while it is true that the spiritual gifts help us function as the Body of Christ, the spiritual gifts *are not for the Body of Christ only.* Did Jesus come to this earth only for the religious and the righteous people? No. As He Himself frequently said, He came for the sick, the sinners, and the sheep of other pastures (Mark 2:17; Luke 5:32; John 10:16). Therefore, since believers are the physical Body of Christ here on earth now, we too must work and serve among the non-Christian, non-religious world.

When you think about your spiritual gifts, don't think about how you can primarily use them to help other Christians. Instead, think about how you can use them to help those who are not Christians. Your spiritual gifts are primarily for the world—not for the church. Christians *are the church* only when we use our spiritual gifts to love and serve the world.

The great benefit to thinking about spiritual gifts this way is that the typical Sunday morning "church service" does not allow most people to use their spiritual gifts. Even when you factor in all of the various ministries and programs of a traditional church, there still are relatively few opportunities for most people to use their spiritual gifts. But this not the case when we avoid this pitfall and start to think about spiritual gifts as an opportunity to be Jesus to others in this world. When we think about spiritual gifts this way, then there is not a lack of opportunity to use our gifts, but a lack of available workers who are willing to go out and love and serve others like Jesus.

So avoid this first general danger of spiritual gifts. They are not primarily for the church. They are given to us so that we can be the church (or be Jesus) to the people of this world.

The second general danger that all spiritual gifts have in common is that each of us tends to think that our gift is the most important one. By their very nature, spiritual gifts cause a person to see the need and importance of their own ways of working with others and serving this world. As a result, however, we fail to see the need and importance of the gifts of other people, and therefore believe that anybody not practicing our spiritual gift is unspiritual. In other words, each person tends to think that their spiritual gift is the most important and that everybody else should be practicing the same thing.

For example, the person with the gift of teaching tends to think that strong biblical preaching and teaching is the most important thing a church can be doing. After all, they think to themselves, if the people don't know God's will and instructions from Scripture, how can they possibly follow and obey Him? And so they place a high emphasis on teaching the Scriptures through meaty sermons on Sunday and frequent Bible study during the week. When someone with the gift of teaching falls into this trap, they start thinking that anybody who doesn't like long, expository sermons is "less spiritual," and anybody who doesn't engage in frequent Bible reading and theological study is possibly not even a Christian.

All the other gifts can fall into the exact same trap. Those with the gifts of mercy or service might think that anybody who does not actively and frequently serve the poor, help the homeless, or provide food for the hungry is less spiritual than those who do. Those with the gift of hospitality might think that those who do not open their home to others are disobedient to God. Those with the gift of giving might think that those who do not generously give to others are being poor stewards of their money.

The solution to this universal problem is to remember what Paul wrote in 1 Corinthians 12, that God has given different spiritual gifts to different people. Each person is supposed to practice their own spiritual gift, and let others practice theirs. Let us not look down on others because they are not practicing our spiritual gifts. Instead, let each of us learn and practice our own spiritual gifts for the benefit of others, while giving them the freedom to do the same with theirs. Only in this way will we all grow in unity, power, and healthy spirituality.

Beyond these two general pitfalls that all the spiritual gifts have in common, there are also some unique dangers that go along with each individual gift. These specific dangers and weakness are considered below.

THE SPECIFIC DANGERS

Administration: Those with the gift of administration can sometimes treat others as if they were employees in a business. Rather than focusing on people and their needs, they might over-prioritize paperwork, "To-Do" lists, and goals. Furthermore, it is easy for someone with the gift of administration to get impatient with people when they do not move fast enough in accomplishing various assigned tasks and duties. Finally, those with the gift of administration sometimes equate their own personal goals and desires with those of God, thereby thinking that anybody who doesn't "get on board" is living contrary to the will of God.

Apostleship (Missionary): Those with the gift of apostleship can fall into the trap of lording their position over others. It is easy for those with the gift of apostleship to confuse their gift with the office of Apostle in the New Testament. When this happens, they tend to portray themselves as authoritative leaders, and then use this position to manipulate and control others for their own ends and purposes. Finally, those who serve as missionaries sometimes give the impression that "real" ministry requires a person to cross an ocean, while forgetting that God just as often calls His people to cross a hallway or a street. It is a sad reality that many of those who cross an ocean to share the gospel with others have never crossed the street to share it with their neighbors.

Craftsmanship: Those with the gift of craftsmanship sometimes think that their gifts are not really spiritual, and therefore, of little help to the Body of Christ. Therefore, they sometimes view their contributions as insignificant or unimportant. It is easy to think that making things with wood or metal does not actually help anyone in their spiritual life. But constructing items that help people live their lives in a community of others and with more ease are important ways of helping others see that God provides for them. These skills also allow the beauty and splendor of God to be magnified on the earth.

Creative Communication: Those with the gift of creative communication must remember that while many often place great emphasis on the written and spoken word, God is a Creator, and has made people to be creative, and so the creative outlets of people help expand and strengthen the Body of Christ in new directions. Of course, since the church often places such an emphasis on the spoken and written word, those with creative communication often get critical of long sermons, deep Bible studies, and advanced theological education. These too are important ways that some people learn. At the same time, they must be patient with those who have trouble finding meaning in art, beauty in music, or symbolic significance in dance.

Celibacy: Those with the gift of celibacy can fall into the trap of judging those who struggle with lust or who need to live with a spouse for companionship and sexual intimacy. Additionally, it is easy for those with the gift of celibacy to look at the problems that married couples face and think that they have the solution. It is quite common for single people to provide unwanted marital advice to couples and parental advice to parents. Those who are not married or do not have children should avoid this urge. Finally, those with the gift of celibacy should not look down upon those who want to spend lots of time with their spouse or children instead of "at church doing ministry." Instead, they must remember that having a good marriage and family is the most central form of Christian ministry and evangelism.

Discernment: Those with the gift of discernment can sometimes be too critical of others. Since they often see faults and weaknesses in others, they might fail to recognize their own failures, or to show mercy to those who struggle. It is also easy for those with the gift of discernment to be overly dogmatic and assertive with their own beliefs and ideas. Therefore, those with the gift of discernment must make an extra effort to listen to the ideas and input of others, while also being patient with those who seem to take a long time to learn or discover truths that seem obvious to them.

Evangelism: Those with the gift of evangelism often feel that everybody should be actively sharing their faith with other people every chance they get. Additionally, they sometimes fail to remember that the best forms of evangelism do not always need to use words. How one lives their life can be a better form of evangelism than taking someone through a gospel tract. Finally, the evangelist must never forget that the task of evangelism does not stop when a person believes in Jesus for eternal life, but has only just begun. True evangelism carries on through discipleship.

Exhortation (Encouragement): Those with the gift of exhortation can sometimes be so focused on encouraging others and creating peace, that they avoid confrontation, even when it is necessary. They can also be too quick to offer advice, sometimes before they actually understand the problem. Furthermore, some with the gift of exhortation fail to understand the perspective and experiences of others before offering advice. As such, their advice can occasionally be simplistic and minimalistic, ignoring the complexity of issues that people often face. To avoid this problem, they must make sure to listen and understand before providing instruction or encouragement. Finally, those with the gift of exhortation or encouragement can be too cheerful and upbeat, even when the circumstances call for sadness. They must remember to mourn with those who mourn and let sorrow complete its cycle.

Faith: Those with the gift of faith often lack patience with those who see the difficulties in various situations, preferring to ignore their objections and instead just move forward, trusting God to work it all out. They need to remember that words of caution and careful planning are also important ways for the people of God to make progress in God's plan and purposes for their lives. Related to this, those with the gift of faith sometimes fall prey to thinking that faith is nothing more than sitting and waiting for God to act. Faith is not "letting go and letting God," but is the persuasion or conviction that God can work in desperate situations, even against impossible odds, but usually in coordination with human activity. So the one who has the gift of faith should listen to the objections offered, and then encourage people to move forward with tangible steps of faith that allow God's power to work and His name to be glorified.

Giving: Those with the gift of giving can sometimes be guilty of condemning or criticizing others who do not seem to give enough. Since those with the gift of giving often give more than 50% of their income away, it is easy for them to be critical of those who give much smaller amounts. Furthermore, since some with the gift of giving are often able to make lots of money, they must watch out for greed. They must remember that even if they give away 50% of their income, the remaining amount is still more than the average person makes. Those with the gift of giving also must ward off the temptation to influence or control how their money is spent when they give it away. The money must be given freely, with no strings or conditions attached. Finally, since their large donations often receive public praise and recognition, it is important that the giver not give in to pride.

Healing: Those with the gift of healing can sometimes go overboard in caring for others. Since the gift of healing can often manifest in providing physical care for others, those who have this gift will sometimes wear themselves out in taking care of others. Beyond this, some people need to learn from their own health mistakes, and so while they can be cared for in their pain and health problems, it is also important to let them experience the pain and hardship from their poor decisions so that they can learn to live healthier in the future. When healing is used in coordination with miracles, those with this gift combination often make the mistake of guaranteeing that someone will be miraculously healed. This can create false hope in others and also bring shame to the name of Jesus Christ if someone dies after they were promised healing. Therefore, those with the gift of healing must never promise that someone will be healed, but should leave all such decisions up to God.

Helping: Those with the gift of helping sometimes think that because they and their work rarely gets recognized, it is not very important. They must remember, however, that their gift of helping others is essential for the proper functioning of other gifts. Another caution for those with this gift is that they have trouble saying "No" to other people who ask for help, and have even greater trouble accepting help from other people. The one with the gift of helps must develop the freedom to say "No" and even to ask others for help when needed. Finally, those with the gift of helping must make sure they help their own family first and foremost. It is easy to see all the needs "out there," while neglecting the needs right within their own household.

Hospitality: Those with the gift of hospitality must ward against the danger of doing little more than entertaining. Hospitality is not simply the ability to make good food and provide a place to sleep for others, but is also the task of making them feel at home and safe. At the same time, the primary responsibility of the person with the gift of hospitality is their own family. It does no good to provide food and lodging for other people if the person's family feels neglected and unsafe in their own home. This is why it is often unwise to welcome complete strangers into one's home while there are still children in the home, as such a use of hospitality can endanger one's own family.

Interpretation of Tongues: Those with the gift of interpretation must be careful to protect themselves against pride when others are amazed at their ability to understand and translate the words of other people. This is especially true when the gift is used in a miraculous way to translate a language that has never been studied. Beyond this, the one with the gift of interpretation should also protect themselves from allowing their own desires or ideas to influence their interpretation. They must always provide an accurate interpretation that is in accordance with the revealed Word of God in Scripture.

Knowledge: Those with the gift of knowledge must watch out for pride (cf. 1 Cor 8:1). It is very easy for the one with knowledge to think that he or she knows more than everyone else, and is therefore correct in everything they teach. They must remain humble and teachable, recognizing that there are unknown flaws in their thinking and holes in their theology. It is important as well for the person with the gift of knowledge to never look down upon those who have little interest in studying Scripture or reading theology. Those with the gift of knowledge often forget that widespread literacy is a recent historical phenomenon, and so they often use Scripture to inflict guilt upon others for not spending plenty of time every day in the study of Scripture. Such Bible study guilt trips must stop.

Leadership: Those with the gift of leadership are often "Type A" personalities who can be abrasive, impatient, abusive, and demanding in their treatment of others. While it is true that those with the gift of leadership often know where people need to go and the steps they need to take to get there, those in leadership positions must be patient with people, leading by example and in love, rather than with fear, manipulation, and control. They must remember that leadership is not loudership, so that the one who is loudest gets to lead. Instead, leadership is loving influence, so that people naturally and willingly follow those who provide and care for them in love.

Martyrdom: Since the person with the gift of martyrdom doesn't really know they have the gift until they are put to death for the cause of Christ, it is difficult for such a person to watch out for their weaknesses. Nevertheless, some people *feel* that they might be asked to give their life for Jesus Christ, and end up being a martyr. In such cases, those who think they have the gift of martyrdom must be wary of thinking that they are being persecuted for Christ just because someone is rude to them. It is quite common for Christians to behave toward others in the meanest and rudest ways imaginable, and then when they receive rude and mean treatment in return, they praise God for being "persecuted for Christ." But this is not what is happening. To the contrary, such Christians are persecuting others in the name of Christ, which is completely contrary to Christ and the gospel. So the primary danger with the gift of martyrdom is in thinking that you have it, and then assuming that others are persecuting you as a result of being a Christian. If you think you have the gift of martyrdom, don't announce it to others or claim that you are being persecuted by others. Instead, suffer silently for the cause of Christ, speaking only when asked to give a reason for the hope that you have (1 Pet 3:14-15).

Mercy: Those with the gift of mercy need to be careful that they do not burn themselves out emotionally. Since they are often dealing with the pain and tragedy in the lives of other people, it is important that they also receive emotional support from others. Of course, it is important for them to recognize as well that God is the ultimate source of comfort, and so while they can help others in their time of need, they must make sure to direct people to God as well, who will never leave them nor forsake them. Finally, those with the gift of mercy must ward themselves against being taken advantage of by others. They are often people-pleasers who want to help everybody who asks, but they need to remember that the best way to help some people is to help them learn from their mistakes and take responsibility for their own actions.

Miracles: Those with the gift of miracles can sometimes fall into the trap of spiritual pride. Since their gift is so awe-inspiring, it is easy for them to turn it into a circus sideshow for wide-eyed onlookers. In other words, the gift of miracles is not for the stage and the crowd, but for the individual person with the need or sickness. Furthermore, the one with the gift of miracles must never promise or guarantee that a miracle will occur. God is the one who sends the miracles, and it is not a sign of "great faith" to promise a sick or dying person that God will make them well. This is instead a sign of little faith, for such a promise reveals a misunderstanding of the nature, character, and power of God. Far too much damage has been done to the cause of Christ by people who promise miracles of healing or financial blessing to others that never come true. So those with the gift of miracles should never make such promises, but should instead allow God to decide when and where miracles occur.

Pastor-Teacher: Those with the gift of pastor-teacher can sometimes develop pride and arrogance, because their ministry often takes place in public venues, in front of adoring crowds. As a result, it is easy for pastor-teachers to take themselves too seriously, forgetting that they are only under-shepherds to the Good Shepherd, Jesus Christ. So the pastor-teacher must remain humble, and must lead, tend, guide, and care for the flock under their care. It is also important to recognize that since the entire church is the flock of God, there must not be competition between individual local churches. There is nothing wrong with a person sitting under the care of one pastor-teacher for a while, and then after a time moving to sit under the care of someone else. As each person matures in their walk with God, they need different types of teaching and encouragement at different times, and so the pastor-teacher must be willing to release people to follow Jesus wherever it is He leads, even if it is to another church or away from Sunday morning gatherings altogether.

Prophecy: Those with the gift of prophecy can sometimes neglect the greater aspect of their gift (the forthtelling of God's will) for the lesser aspect (foretelling the future) because the latter is more spectacular. So the person with the gift of prophecy must maintain the correct balance, as did the Prophets of Scripture, by spending most of their time calling people away from sin and back to obedience. At the same time, however, the prophet must make their call to repentance with love and mercy. They should seek to protect themselves from being too harsh or critical toward others when their sin is pointed out, or too impatient when people do not repent or change as quickly as the prophet expects. The prophetic call must reflect the heart of God, which is full of tender, loving care, and limitless patience for His straying children.

Service: Those with the gift of service might be tempted to think that their gift is not very important, since they rarely receive any praise or recognition from others. It is also easy for those with the gift of service to let themselves be taken advantage of by others, taking on too much work. Therefore, the servant should set boundaries, protecting their time and energy, so they can provide quality service over a longer period of time for those who truly need it. Finally, since the needs of others are vast and varied and can become all-consuming, the servant must always remember to serve at home first. The servant must not neglect their family while in the service of others.

Teaching: Those with the gift of teaching can sometimes get bogged down with insignificant details of the biblical text or the theological topic they are studying, so that what they teach to others has very little practical application for people's daily lives. Therefore, the one who teaches should always try to make their teaching relevant and applicable to life. Also, the one who teaches must always be learning as well, for the best teachers are also teachable. A teachable person is humble and inquisitive, so that they always have fresh ideas and new insights to teach to others (cf. 2 Tim 2:2).

Tongues: Those with the gift of tongues must first of all make sure they actually have it. Since tongues is sought after by so many people in the church, many people think they have the gift of tongues when they really do not. Related to this, many who have the gift of tongues are tempted to use it as a way to make themselves look more spiritual in the eyes of others. Therefore, the one with the gift of tongues should never speak in a public setting in a showy or dramatic way, and especially when there is no interpreter present.

Voluntary Poverty: Those with the gift of voluntary poverty often struggle with the consumerism and materialism that pervades the surrounding culture, church, and other Christians. It is easy, therefore, to condemn and criticize others who spend money on cars, houses, clothes, or vacations when there is so much poverty, hunger, and sickness in the world. The one who has chosen the life of voluntary poverty should remember that not all are called to this same lifestyle, and so it is not wrong or sinful for other Christians to enjoy some of the blessings of God's creation.

Wisdom: Those with the gift of wisdom tend to become very frustrated at the foolish choices, decisions, and lifestyles of other people. They can also struggle with selfishness, as they tend to make decisions that benefit themselves personally in their jobs, finances, and relationships. Therefore, the one with the gift of wisdom should treat others with patience and love, providing counsel and insight into the types of decisions they can make which will help their life turn out for the best. They must remember that what appears to them as "common sense" is not commonly known to other people.

As you read the warnings above for your spiritual gifts, you might have recognized some things you struggle with and some things you don't. This is okay. As stated previously, not everyone struggles with the same things in each gift, and the best thing you can do with your spiritual gift is practice and experiment with it as you serve others and edify the Body of Christ. As you do this, you will strengthen the effectiveness of your spiritual gift while avoiding some of its weaknesses. So keep practicing and ministering, so that the entire church will be knit together in unity and love until we all come to the fullness of Jesus Christ.

Most of all, use your gifts so that the world can reap the benefits of these gifts. Jesus came to love and serve the world, and as followers of Jesus, we must do the same. We must seek to show God's love to a lost and hurting world.

But this raises a question. You might have heard that some of the spiritual gifts are no longer in use. Is this true? This is the question we consider next.

CHAPTER 7

HAVE SOME OF THE GIFTS CEASED?

There are many within Christianity who believe and teach that various spiritual gifts have ceased to be given by God or practiced by the church. Those who hold this view believe that some of the "sign" gifts such as tongues, prophecy, miracles, and healing were important for the birth and initial expansion of the church, but once the church was founded, these sorts of gifts faded away from use.

Various arguments are given in support of this idea. For example, some look at the frequent accounts of tongues, miracles, and healing in the Book of Acts, and then look at the relative infrequent use of such things today, and conclude that something must have changed between then and now. But of course, the frequency of such miraculous events depends entirely on who you ask. Certain groups claim that prophecy, tongues, and miracles are even *more common* today than they were in the Book of Acts. So this argument for the cessation of certain gifts is somewhat arbitrary.

Some people also point to Jesus' statement in Matthew 12 that only a wicked and adulterous generation asks for a sign (Matt 12:39). Since these so-called "sign gifts" are often sought out by large audiences of relatively new Christians, some apply Jesus' statements from Matthew 12 to the similar crowds today who only seem to seek after signs. While the warning is probably appropriate, the fact that people seek signs doesn't necessarily mean that the "signs gifts" have ceased. It just means that people can abuse them, both then and now.

The main reason some think various gifts have ceased is because of what Paul wrote in 1 Corinthians 13:8-13. He said that prophecy will fail and tongues will cease when "that which is perfect has come" (1 Cor 13:8-13). Some people see this as a reference to the birthing of the church and its expansion around the world. Once the church was fully formed in the first century, there was no longer any need for some of the foundational and miraculous gifts. Therefore, these gifts ceased to function.

But this view has several problems. For example, along with prophecy and tongues, Paul also lists knowledge (1 Cor 13:8). Few who believe that tongues and prophecy have ceased also believe that knowledge has ceased. To the contrary, nearly all Christians believe that the spiritual gift of knowledge is very much in use today. So why would tongues and prophesy cease while

knowledge did not, when Paul mentions all three together?

Another problem, of course, is that Paul does not
explain what he means when he writes about "that
which is perfect." But whatever he meant, it doesn't
seem logical that he would have meant the coming of
the church. After all, the church had already been born
by the time Paul wrote this. And if Paul meant that
these gifts would end when the church spread over the
entire earth, this still hasn't happened in our own day,
which means the gifts should still be in effect.

The most likely explanation of Paul's statement,
therefore, is that he was thinking of the perfect future
state that will exist in the new heavens and new earth
after the old have passed away and God makes everything new (Rev 21:1-5). The new heavens and new
earth will be different and better than this current sin-
filled planet we live in. As a result, how we live and
work together as humans will also be different, and so
there will be no need for any of the spiritual gifts. I as-
sume that we will each still have different interests, hobbies, and talents, but God has not provided many details
about our future eternal existence, and so we must be
careful about making assumptions. The bottom line is
that as long as we are on this earth and in these non-
perfect bodies, all the spiritual gifts will be in use.

This doesn't necessarily mean that when someone
claims to be speaking in tongues, giving a prophecy, or

healing the sick, they are actually doing so. Due to the nature of spiritual gifts, they can be easily abused or faked. This is, in fact, one of the reasons that some people think some of the gifts have cased. When they see how some gifts are misunderstood, misapplied, and abused, they want to correct these problems, and the easiest way to do so is to simply claim that the gifts have ceased functioning.

It is indeed true that some groups twist and distort various spiritual gifts (such as tongues, prophecies, and miracles) so that they are used to put on a "magic" show in front of large audiences. This is not the way spiritual gifts were ever used in the Bible, and is not the way such gifts are to be used today. But the solution is not to ban the gifts or say they have ceased from use, for this would only bring harm to the rest of the Body (1 Cor 12:21, 25-26). The solution to the abuse of spiritual gifts is to properly understand what they are (and are not), and how to use them for the edification of others, while also avoiding the problems which the gifts can cause.

It is also critical to understand that while all the gifts are still in use, some of the gifts (such as apostleship and tongues) have changed in how they are implemented within the Body of Christ. ultimately, when properly understood and practiced, we conclude that all the spiritual gifts are still in use today, including those of apostleship, healing, miracles, and tongues.

Nevertheless, since so many people have questions

about the gift of tongues, let me briefly try to address some of the main issues related to this confusing spiritual gift.

CHAPTER 8

WHAT ABOUT TONGUES?

The gift of tongues is a tricky topic. Most Christians have strong opinions about it one way or the other. Some think it was in use in the early church era but has now completely ceased, while others think it is a gift that all Christians should practice as a means to spiritual growth. Some think it is a gift that can be taught and learned, while others say it is only miraculously received. The following short chapter on tongues will not solve all these differences, but will hopefully provide a middle-ground perspective that will create some peace between the opposing sides while also giving a brief explanation for how the gift of tongues is presented in Scripture.

TONGUES IN THE OLD TESTAMENT

The main point to recognize regarding tongues is that the New Testament is not the first place they are mentioned. Speaking in tongues is first referenced in various places in the Old Testament. Genesis 11 reveals that

God judged the people building the tower to the heavens by causing people to speak in different tongues so that they could not understand each other. As a result of this divine discipline, the people spread out over the face of the earth. This first use of tongues in the Bible reveals a theme that is found elsewhere as well. People speaking in other tongues is a symbolic sign of divine discipline which leads to the scattering and dispersion of the people. This same cycle is found elsewhere in the Old Testament where speaking in foreign tongues is mentioned (cf. Deut 28:15, 49, 64-65; Isa 28:9-13; 33:19; Jer 5:15, 19).

So the consistent theme in all these texts is that speaking in tongues is a sign to the Jewish people that God's divine discipline is coming, and that if they do not change their ways, they will be scattered and dispersed upon the earth. And this is exactly what happened following the ministry of Jesus. He announced that God's kingdom was coming, but most Jewish people rejected Jesus as the Messiah. So following the death, resurrection, and ascension of Jesus, the Jews in Jerusalem at Pentecost heard others speaking in tongues (Acts 2:4, 8). The Jewish people were then scattered and dispersed in AD 70 after Jerusalem and the temple were destroyed by the Roman Empire.[3]

The first point to recognize about tongues, therefore, is that they are not a sign of God's blessing, but a sign of God's discipline. They serve as a warning about impending destruction and dispersion. Why does God send the warning this way? It is so that the people who hear the warning in other languages know that the message is not of human origin, but comes directly from God. In Isaiah 28, for example, the Jewish people criticize Isaiah for saying the same thing to them over and over and over. They mock Isaiah as if he were a child. The statement in Isaiah 28:13 could be translated as "But the word of the Lord to them was, 'Blah blah blah yada yada yada.'" It is with this sort of scornful mockery that they criticized Isaiah's words.[4]

This is why God said that He will send foreigners to speak to the Jews in another tongue (Isa 28:11). The implication is that when they hear the translation of these other words, they will discover that these others are saying the same thing Isaiah said. This would prove that the message was from God, for foreigners would not have collaborated with the prophet to speak the same message he had spoken. If, therefore, the Jewish

[3] For a good summary of this view, see George W. Zeller, *God's Gift of Tongues* (Eugene OR: Wipf & Stock, 1978), 77-90. He goes on to argue that as a result of the dispersion, tongues has ceased. But this does not necessarily follow, for there were several cycles of tongues and dispersion prior to the events of Acts. Therefore, it seems logical that the cycle could repeat after AD 70 as well.

[4] See my book, *Cruciform Pastoral Leadership* (Dallas, OR: Redeeming Press, 2019), for further explanation of Isaiah 28:13.

people did not respond either to the message of Isaiah or the message spoken in a foreign tongue, this would then lead to scattering and dispersion. And this is exactly what has happened over and over throughout Israelite history.

TONGUES ARE HUMAN LANGUAGES

Following this truth about the biblical nature and purpose of tongues, we also learn that biblical tongues are always a human language. Most of the biblical texts that describe tongues also point out that the tongues are other human languages (cf. Gen 11:7-9; Deut 28:49; Isa 28:9-13; 33:19; Jer 5:15; Acts 2:6, 8). Also, the fact that Paul writes in 1 Corinthians 14 that tongues should never be spoken unless an interpreter is present indicates that tongues are an actual human language which can be interpreted. There is no evidence in Scripture anywhere that tongues is a "heavenly" or "angelic" language that sounds like gibberish.

As a side note, the texts of Romans 8:26 and Jude 20 are likely not referring to speaking in tongues. Both of these texts refer to "praying in the Spirit" and Paul even mentions praying with "groaning which cannot be uttered" (Rom 8:26). But neither of these texts mention anything about tongues, and so they should be taken literally, as having nothing to do with speaking in another language. Sometimes, when people pray, they struggle with knowing what words to use, or even how to pray for a certain situation. In such cases, trust the Holy Spirit to give you the actual words you should say (this is praying in the Spirit ... with an actual language you understand), and in some cases, to maybe even pray without words at all, but instead with emotional utterances of groans and sighs. These groans and sighs are not words, but are the same sort of sounds anyone might make in times of deep physical pain, mental need, or emotional distress. So these texts are not referring to speaking in tongues. In Scripture, tongues always refers to speaking another human language.

TONGUES AS A SIGN OF THE KINGDOM

One final line of evidence to understand about the gift of tongues is how it is related to the spread of the gospel in the Book of Acts. It is critical to recognize that the Book of Acts does not describe the perfect church in the way God wanted it to be forevermore, but instead describes the birth of the church and its initial growth upon the earth. If the church were a human being, the Book of Acts would describe its infancy years. But just as a human must grow up and mature, so also must the church. The Book of Acts, therefore, does not offer a prescription for how the church should behave, but simply offers a description of how the early church was born and began to function.

At the beginning, Jesus instructed the disciples to carry the gospel to the ends of the earth, beginning in Jerusalem, Judea, and Samaria (Acts 1:8). They were to spread the rule and reign of God (i.e., the Kingdom of God), as inaugurated and exemplified by Jesus, to the ends of the earth. And Peter himself was given the keys of the kingdom for this very purpose (Matt 16:19). So it was Peter's responsibility to unlock the door of the Kingdom to the various people groups on earth. This was to begin with the Jews in Jerusalem and Judea, and then spread outward to the Samaritans and the Gentiles. And this is indeed exactly what happens in the Book of Acts.

After Jesus ascended, the disciples were in the Upper Room when the Holy Spirit came upon them, and many of them started speaking in tongues (Acts 2:5-8). Peter was present, and he explained to the multitude what was happening and what it meant (Acts 2:14-39). In Acts 8, the gospel spreads to the Samaritans (Acts 8:4-8). But note that nobody in Samaria received the Holy Spirit (and presumably started speaking in tongues, though the text doesn't say this) until Peter arrived and "unlocked the door of the Kingdom" to the Samaritans by laying hands on them (Acts 8:14-17).

Later, Peter is similarly instructed by God to preach the gospel to a Gentile convert to Judaism, Cornelius (Acts 10:1-16). So Peter goes and after he preaches the gospel to them, Cornelius and his household receive the

Holy Spirit and start speaking in tongues (Acts 10:33-48). This indicates that the door to the Kingdom had now been flung open to the Gentiles as well. Peter's task was finished, and we do not hear much more about Peter in the Book of Acts.

However, the church debated whether or not the gospel could truly be preached to the Gentiles. Though Paul was traveling around the Roman Empire preaching Jesus and proclaiming peace to all (Acts 13ff), not all Jewish Christians were convinced that all Gentiles were welcome. For although Cornelius had been a Gentile, he had converted to Judaism, and so many Jews believed that before a Gentile could accept the gospel and believe in Jesus, they must first convert to Judaism. This is what the church leaders discussed in Acts 15. So when Paul encountered a group of Gentiles in Ephesus who had heard bits and pieces of the gospel, he laid hands on them so that they might receive the Holy Spirit. When they did, they also began to speak in tongues (Acts 19:1-6). Paul was able to do this because Peter had already unlocked the door to the Gentiles. Paul's actions only confirmed that the door was indeed unlocked to any and all who would believe.

Other than these incidents, we do not hear about the gift of tongues in the Book of Acts. It is only mentioned in these critical transitionary accounts which show the fulfillment of Jesus' instructions in Acts 1:8. In each case, the gift of tongues was a sign to the Jewish leaders that God's discipline was coming, which would be followed by a dispersion, and therefore, the gospel of Jesus Christ should be spread far and wide so that the church as the people of God on earth might survive and thrive. In this case, the dispersion had been redeemed by God, so that it was no longer a form of discipline and judgment. It became a form of blessing, as it showed that God was working in the world to reverse Babel and spread the Gospel far and wide within the seeds of the scattered church.

TONGUES AND 1 CORINTHIANS 14

All of these ideas about tongues are reinforced by what Paul writes in 1 Corinthians 12–14. He points out that tongues are a sign (1 Cor 14:21-22). The unbelievers he mentioned are not general unbelievers of the world, but unbelieving *Jews* as indicated by Paul's quote from Isaiah 28:11-12. He also indicates that tongues are a spoken human language when he indicates that there must be a translation if someone speaks in another tongue during a church gathering (1 Cor 14:6-19). And of course, the ultimate goal is love (1 Cor 13) and edification of the Body (1 Cor 14:1-5). Paul even states that he would rather speak 10,000 words that can be understood by himself and others than 5 words which cannot be understood (1 Cor 14:19).

The spread of the gospel and the advancement of the

Kingdom requires that what we say be understood by those who hear it. The bottom line truth about tongues, therefore, is that if a person speaks in tongues, it must be translated so that those who hear are instructed and edified. Otherwise, where there is no understanding, there is no benefit to the one who speaks or the one who hears (1 Cor 14:15-17). Note that according to Paul, even the one who speaks in tongues is not edified by tongues if he or she does not know what they are saying. Even the personal use of tongues requires a translation if it is going to be helpful and beneficial to the speaker (1 Cor 14:13).

ARE TONGUES FOR TODAY?

Due to the transitionary and redemptive use of tongues in the Book of Acts, it appears that the gift of tongues might very well be in use today. However, whenever and wherever God allows this gift to be used, the basic principles of tongues still stand. Tongues are always a human language that is spoken to a group of people as a way of introducing them to the gospel and indicating the truthfulness and divine origin of what is said. Therefore, when an interpreter is not present, tongues serve no purpose, and the speaker should remain silent (1 Cor 14:28).

So I think that the gift of tongues could still be in use today, albeit in a slightly different way than commonly practiced in many modern church gatherings, and also somewhat different than the way it is used and described in Scripture. The Old Testament use of tongues was a sign to the Jewish people that God was disciplining them for their failure to hear and respond to His message. In these situations, God sent an identical message to what the prophets had preached, but He sent it through people who spoke another language. If the Jewish people still did not hear and respond, then further discipline would come in the form of scattering and dispersion.

But in the Book of Acts, while the gift of tongues still served as a sign to Jewish people that discipline and judgment were coming, it also helped spread the gospel to other people groups, showing the Jewish people and the world that the Kingdom of God was open to all. This transitionary and redemptive use of tongues helps us understand how tongues might be in use today.

Since we no longer need evidence or proof (the way the early Jewish Christians did) that the gospel is available to all people around the world we should not expect to see the widespread use of tongues as a sign to verify that the door to the Kingdom of God has been opened to these other groups. We know it is open, and we don't need a sign to prove it. Therefore, the only remaining purpose for the use of tongues is to help spread the gospel message of Jesus to those who have not yet heard it in their own language.

If the gift of tongues is in use today, it would be used in evangelistic settings where the speaker is specially gifted by God to speak in another language (or quickly learn another language) for the sake of sharing the gospel message with others. This is how it was used in Acts 2, and it appears that this might be what Paul was referring to in 1 Corinthians 14 when he wrote about speaking in tongues more than anyone else (1 Cor 14:18). Paul's evangelistic and missionary travels likely put him in situations where he needed to convey the gospel message to people who spoke other languages. The gift of tongues enabled him to do so.

So do you think you have the gift of tongues? If so, don't use it for personal reasons, and also don't think that this gift somehow makes you more spiritual than others. All the gifts are equally important for the health and growth of the Body. Instead, pray that God will help you use your ability to speak in other languages so that those who have not heard the gospel will come to understand it and believe in Jesus for eternal life. Though tongues is one of the "stranger" gifts, go ahead and embrace your strangeness for Jesus, as all of us should do with the gifts we have been given.

CHAPTER 9

EMBRACE YOUR GIFTS

The beautiful thing about spiritual gifts is that they make you unique. Due to your spiritual gift mix (along with your abilities, desires, talents, experience, and skills), there is nobody else in the world who is just like you, nor will there ever be. This is incredibly liberating when you think about it.

Most people in this world spend large amounts of time trying to act like everyone else. They try to behave like the popular kids at school, talk like the actors on TV, dress like the sports stars on the playing field, and look like the pretty people in the magazines. But we can never be someone else … and they can never be us. Each person is completely and majestically unique. And until you recognize and embrace this, you will always struggle in this life. You will always fail at trying to measure up. You will always feel insignificant and over-looked.

But once you embrace who God made you to be, you will then be set free to be as strange and unique as you possibly can. You will begin to realize that since nobody can ever be you, you might as well be the best you that you can be. This comes by embracing your quirks, reveling in your differences, and strengthening the things that make you stand out in a crowd. Learning and using your spiritual gifts allows you to become and "own" who you are.

THE FRUSTRATION OF CONFORMITY

A few years ago my wife and I had a conversation in which we both discovered that we were each trying to be the other person. My wife, Wendy, is a lover and a server. She is very passionate and emotional. She nearly always speaks and acts before she thinks. Whatever she does, she dives in head first and with both feet. I don't know how she does this, since it's logically impossible, but she does. Logic has never stopped Wendy from doing the impossible. I, on the other hand, am a thinker and a writer. I am even-keeled to the point of being emotionless. I never speak unless I have thought through what I am going to say and all the possible ways the other person might respond. I tend to approach everything logically, as if it were a puzzle to be solved. I tend to prefer books over people.

For many years in our marriage, I felt terribly guilty that I did not spend enough time getting to know our neighbors, taking baked-goods over to friends, or playing with children down at the park the way my wife did.

I thought that a "true" follower of Jesus would be out volunteering at the soup-kitchen, chatting with the neighbors about tomato-growing tips, and learning the names of the children down at the local park. I used to think that a "true" follower of Jesus would go about with a spirit and attitude of prayer and grace as they spend their days washing, serving, scrubbing, praying, befriending, and talking.

But that was never me. Not ever.

Within a week of moving into a new neighborhood, my wife has taken fresh-baked loaves of bread and cookies to our neighbors and has had hour-long conversations with all of them, learning about their dogs, their jobs, and their children. When I talk to the neighbors, however, I am barely able to talk about anything more than the weather. I fear going to get the mail, because I am afraid I will meet a neighbor. I dread running into a coworker at Wal-Mart because I will probably forget their name or not know what to say.

If Wendy goes to the local park, she will have a crowd of children around her in ten minutes, all of them laughing, cheering, and giggling. In a few minutes more, she will know their names. She will know their dog's names. They even ask her when she is coming back to the park. I call her a modern-day Pied Piper (but in a good way). When I have tried this in the past, I am pretty sure I scared the kids. I know I scared the parents, because when they saw a long-haired strange man trying to talk nicely to their children, they immediately call the kids over because "It's time to go home!" I am not making this up.

When Wendy stands in line at the grocery store, people just talk to her about things. Sometimes, she strikes up conversations with them, but more often than not, they start conversations with her. This has never happened to me. Not once in my entire life. Nobody ever starts a conversation with me at the grocery store. I have tried to start a conversation with others, and they usually look at me like I'm some sort of freak.

So it was a shock for me to discover a few years back that my wife felt just as guilty as I did, but about the opposite things. While she was great with people, she felt guilty that she wasn't spending as much time studying Scripture and reading theology as I did. She saw me reading a couple theology books per week and studying several hours each day, and felt that she wasn't spending enough time "in the Word." She feared that she wasn't being "spiritual" enough to be a strong Christian. After all, she attended the same Bible College I did, where we learned that "disciple" means "student, pupil, learner." As a result, she thought that if she was a fully-committed disciple of Jesus Christ, she needed to be studying and learning every day.

In fact, during our first ten years of marriage, while I was a pastor, my wife tried to wear the "Bible and theology student hat." She attended every Bible study, every theology conference, and made sure she read and studied the Bible every day. It slowly killed her, for all of this study and reading kept her from having time to love and serve other people. She stopped all of her people-focused activities to make sure she had adequate time to become the "disciple-student" that good Christians were supposed to become. It wasn't until years later when we followed Jesus out of institutional Christianity that she felt the freedom to focus more on people than on Bible study. But she still felt guilty for not spending more time studying the way I was.

So when we discovered that each of us was trying to be the other person, it is then that we realized that both of us were perfect just as we were. We realized that God made Wendy to be Wendy, and He made me to be me. We also realized that rather than fight who God made us to be, we must instead revel in it. Best of all, since we are married, we can work together as a team to both do the things that each of us is uniquely suited to do.

Wendy shines when we have people over to our house. She almost literally glows, especially when the company includes children. I swear that I sometimes see beams of light coming out of her eyes and smile. She is specially gifted by God to love and serve others with her whole being. She bakes, cooks, talks, serves, and loves people in a way I have never seen anybody else match.

I, on the other hand, will sit for hours with my nose in a pile of books, chasing down insights into various

Greek words, information about the historical background of a biblical event, and ideas about how to understand a particular text. This reasoning ability also allows me to fix problems around the house. I have often dismantled and then fixed lawn mowers and dishwashers. I built a state-of-the-art chicken coop, complete with heated water and a slide-out cleaning tray, simply by looking at a picture online. I taught myself to design and code websites, create and sell books, and publish a Bible study podcast and online theology courses.

Wendy looks at me and says, "How can you sit and study so long? How can you know what needs to be fixed on the dishwasher?" I look at her and say, "How can you love to bake and entertain children so often?" And for many years, when each of us tried to be the other person, both of us were miserable. But now that we have recognized that each of us has specific gifts, talents, strengths, and abilities, and that we are each supposed to strengthen, develop, and use our *own* gifts (rather than those of someone else), life has become much more enjoyable. And so has our marriage.

Since we are married, I get to join Wendy as she cooks and converses with friends and neighbors. By myself, I could never do this. But I am happy to join her when she does it. And Wendy gets to hear my ideas and insight into Scripture as we discuss what is going on inside my head. As different as we are, we need each other, and we help each other do things that we could not do on our own. I need her to lead me in practical ways to put my ideas into practice, and she needs me to help theologically affirm and encourage her actions in loving others. We learned to accept who God made us to be. We learned that it was better to revel in our strengths than to resist them.

The Olympic runner, Eric Liddell, once said, "I believe God made me for a purpose, but he also made me fast. And when I run I feel His pleasure." My wife feels God's pleasure when she bakes for other people, plays with children, ministers to the neighbors, and laughs with friends. I feel God's pleasure when I discover something new about a certain Greek word, when I read an intriguing idea in someone else's book, or when I am able to help someone in their Christian life by answering a tricky theological question. My wife is not me, and she shouldn't try to be me. Similarly, I am not my wife, and shouldn't try to be her. Yet we both need each other. I do the studying for her and she learns from me. She does the love and service and helps me make friends and love others in ways I could never do on my own.

BE WHO YOU ARE

The same thing is true for you. God made you to be who you are. So embrace it! Discover your gifts, throw caution to the wind, and fling yourself into your strange, unique life with wild abandon. Rather than seeking to become a clone of somebody else, become who God uniquely gifted you to be. Only then will you find satisfaction in life and fulfillment in this world. Only then will the Body of Christ develop in healthy and beautiful ways as you contribute as only you can.

Of course, you must let others do the same. Just as each of us must be who God made us to be, we must allow others to be whom God made them to be. I must not expect others to tirelessly read and study, and they must not expect me to be invigorated by baking a cake or listening to our neighbor talk about his dog. Imagine the beauty and glory that would enter into this world if we all embraced our gifts and allowed others to do the same? It is only because of this beautiful diversity that the church exists in this world. The beauty of Christianity is not that we are all the same or that we are all "balanced," but instead, that we are all so dissimilar and opposite, and that in Christ, we are unified and can celebrate the differences and insanities of others rather than calling them to "become like us."

So don't try to be balanced. Don't try to fit in. Don't try to be someone else. Be the best "you" that you can be, for you cannot be anyone else, and nobody else can be "you" either. God created you to do something, so go do it! Don't turn to the left or the right by pious-sounding talk about wearing the "right" clothes, using the "right" language, hanging out with the "right" people, or acting in the "right" way. Instead, find your divine spark of "madness" and fully embrace it until it turns into a raging inferno. Then people will come from miles away just to watch you burn.

EMBRACE YOUR INSANITY

When you live the way God made you to live, some people might think you're insane. At times, you might agree with them. But learn to accept your insanity. Embrace it. Enjoy it. Live it. Be different and be proud.

I dive fully into reading, writing, and studying. This is why people are often amazed at how I publish 2-3 books per year. But that's my insanity and I love it. My wife is always full-steam ahead with cooking and helping others. It is so insane sometimes, that I tell my daughters, "Remember ... when you grow up and become a mother, you don't have to do everything your mother does in order to be a good mother. She's insane."

What is your insanity? What are the passions, interests, and gifts that make you "you"? Fling yourself into these whole-heartedly for your own satisfaction and for the glory of God. As you exercise you spiritual gifts, you might find yourself neck-deep in one of the following areas:

- Loving your family and friends

- Caring for children
- Cooking, baking, and hospitality
- Ministry to prostitutes
- Providing for the homeless
- Serving the elderly
- Conserving nature
- Tending to animals
- Involving yourself in politics
- Studying and teaching Scripture
- Learning and writing about theology
- Helping others live a healthy life
- Giving generously to others
- Cleaning your town and neighborhood
- Researching medical and scientific advances
- Healing the sick and injured
- And millions of other possibilities

By learning about your spiritual gifts and choosing to put them into practice, you will be allowing God to form and shape you into the amazing and astonishing person He made you to be. Embrace your gifts and let the world see the light and the glory of God shining through you.

SPIRITUAL GIFTS INVENTORY

Instructions for Use:

1. There are a total of 125 statements below. For each statement, circle whether you *Strongly Agree, Somewhat Agree,* are *Undecided, Somewhat Disagree,* or *Completely Disagree.* Try to use *Undecided* no more than five times.

2. When you have completed all 125 statements, transfer your answers to the profile sheet at the end of this document.

3. Total your scores for each of the gifts. Each gift will have a score between ZERO and TWENTY.

4. Order the gifts in descending order of score. Higher scores indicate your more dominant gifts.

5. For more information on your gift and how to use it, look at the chapter titled "What Are the Spiritual Gifts?"

1) *I enjoy the responsibility of making important decisions that affect others.*

> 4-Strongly Agree
> 3-Somewhat Agree
> 2-Undecided
> 1-Somewhat Disagree
> 0-Completely Disagree

2) *I often think God is calling me to take the gospel to people who haven't heard about Jesus.*

> 4-Strongly Agree
> 3-Somewhat Agree
> 2-Undecided
> 1-Somewhat Disagree
> 0-Completely Disagree

3) *I enjoy working creatively with wood, cloth, paints, metal, glass, or other materials.*

> 4-Strongly Agree
> 3-Somewhat Agree
> 2-Undecided
> 1-Somewhat Disagree
> 0-Completely Disagree

4) *I enjoy developing and using my artistic skills (art,*

drama, music, photography, etc.).

4-Strongly Agree

3-Somewhat Agree

2-Undecided

1-Somewhat Disagree

0-Completely Disagree

5) *It is easy for me to recognize talents and gifts in other people.*

4-Strongly Agree

3-Somewhat Agree

2-Undecided

1-Somewhat Disagree

0-Completely Disagree

6) *I live out the truths of gospel with words and actions so that others see and understand God's love and grace in their lives.*

4-Strongly Agree

3-Somewhat Agree

2-Undecided

1-Somewhat Disagree

0-Completely Disagree

7) *It is enjoyable to motivate people to help them take the*

next step in following Jesus.

> 4-Strongly Agree
> 3-Somewhat Agree
> 2-Undecided
> 1-Somewhat Disagree
> 0-Completely Disagree

8) *I often step out to attempt the impossible.*

> 4-Strongly Agree
> 3-Somewhat Agree
> 2-Undecided
> 1-Somewhat Disagree
> 0-Completely Disagree

9) *I give liberally and joyfully to people in financial need or to projects requiring support.*

> 4-Strongly Agree
> 3-Somewhat Agree
> 2-Undecided
> 1-Somewhat Disagree
> 0-Completely Disagree

10) *I often know what is wrong with people physically, and know what steps are needed to help them recover to full health.*

4-Strongly Agree
3-Somewhat Agree
2-Undecided
1-Somewhat Disagree
0-Completely Disagree

11) *I enjoy working behind the scenes in order to support the work of others.*

4-Strongly Agree
3-Somewhat Agree
2-Undecided
1-Somewhat Disagree
0-Completely Disagree

12) *I view my home as a place to love and serve other people.*

4-Strongly Agree
3-Somewhat Agree
2-Undecided
1-Somewhat Disagree
0-Completely Disagree

13) *I often wonder why people struggle with sexual urges, since these are not a temptation for me.*

4-Strongly Agree

3-Somewhat Agree

2-Undecided

1-Somewhat Disagree

0-Completely Disagree

14) *It is easy for me to learn foreign languages.*

4-Strongly Agree

3-Somewhat Agree

2-Undecided

1-Somewhat Disagree

0-Completely Disagree

15) *I am often approached by people who want to know my perspective on a certain Bible passage or theological concept.*

4-Strongly Agree

3-Somewhat Agree

2-Undecided

1-Somewhat Disagree

0-Completely Disagree

16) *I am able to motivate others to accomplish a goal.*

4-Strongly Agree

3-Somewhat Agree

2-Undecided

1-Somewhat Disagree

0-Completely Disagree

17) *I empathize with hurting people and desire to help in their healing process.*

4-Strongly Agree

3-Somewhat Agree

2-Undecided

1-Somewhat Disagree

0-Completely Disagree

18) *I very frequently see God miraculously alter circumstances when I pray.*

4-Strongly Agree

3-Somewhat Agree

2-Undecided

1-Somewhat Disagree

0-Completely Disagree

19) *My wallet and bank account are nearly always empty because I give so much money away.*

4-Strongly Agree

3-Somewhat Agree

2-Undecided

1-Somewhat Disagree

0-Completely Disagree

20) *It is enjoyable to have the responsibility of leading other people in their spiritual life.*

4-Strongly Agree

3-Somewhat Agree

2-Undecided

1-Somewhat Disagree

0-Completely Disagree

21) *I often speak in a way that results in conviction and a change of life in others.*

4-Strongly Agree

3-Somewhat Agree

2-Undecided

1-Somewhat Disagree

0-Completely Disagree

22) *There is great joy in doing little jobs for other people and helping with day-to-day tasks.*

4-Strongly Agree

3-Somewhat Agree

2-Undecided

1-Somewhat Disagree

0-Completely Disagree

23) *I love to read and study God's Word and then share with others what I have learned.*

    4-Strongly Agree
    3-Somewhat Agree
    2-Undecided
    1-Somewhat Disagree
    0-Completely Disagree

24) *Sometimes I am able to speak to a person in their own language even though I have never studied it.*

    4-Strongly Agree
    3-Somewhat Agree
    2-Undecided
    1-Somewhat Disagree
    0-Completely Disagree

25) *I am often sought out for advice on personal or spiritual matters.*

    4-Strongly Agree
    3-Somewhat Agree
    2-Undecided
    1-Somewhat Disagree
    0-Completely Disagree

26) *I enjoy organizing people and harnessing their gifts and talents to solve a particular problem.*

> 4-Strongly Agree
> 3-Somewhat Agree
> 2-Undecided
> 1-Somewhat Disagree
> 0-Completely Disagree

27) *I have a strong burden to share the gospel with the unreached people groups of the world.*

> 4-Strongly Agree
> 3-Somewhat Agree
> 2-Undecided
> 1-Somewhat Disagree
> 0-Completely Disagree

28) *I am skilled in working with different kinds of tools.*

> 4-Strongly Agree
> 3-Somewhat Agree
> 2-Undecided
> 1-Somewhat Disagree
> 0-Completely Disagree

29) *I use art, plays, pictures, or music to help people un-*

derstand God, themselves, this world, and their relation-ships.

> 4-Strongly Agree
> 3-Somewhat Agree
> 2-Undecided
> 1-Somewhat Disagree
> 0-Completely Disagree

30) *I usually detect spiritual truth from spiritual error before fellow believers.*

> 4-Strongly Agree
> 3-Somewhat Agree
> 2-Undecided
> 1-Somewhat Disagree
> 0-Completely Disagree

31) *I find it easier to build relationships with non-believers than with believers.*

> 4-Strongly Agree
> 3-Somewhat Agree
> 2-Undecided
> 1-Somewhat Disagree
> 0-Completely Disagree

32) *I like to encourage people to revitalize their spiritual*

life through Bible study, prayer, or getting involved in community service.

> 4-Strongly Agree
> 3-Somewhat Agree
> 2-Undecided
> 1-Somewhat Disagree
> 0-Completely Disagree

33) *I find it natural and easy to know that God is hearing and answering my prayers.*

> 4-Strongly Agree
> 3-Somewhat Agree
> 2-Undecided
> 1-Somewhat Disagree
> 0-Completely Disagree

34) *I manage my money well in order to free more of it for giving.*

> 4-Strongly Agree
> 3-Somewhat Agree
> 2-Undecided
> 1-Somewhat Disagree
> 0-Completely Disagree

35) *When someone is sick or injured, I pray for them and*

check up on them until they recover.

4-Strongly Agree

3-Somewhat Agree

2-Undecided

1-Somewhat Disagree

0-Completely Disagree

36) *In life, I gravitate toward undone work, even if unpopular.*

4-Strongly Agree

3-Somewhat Agree

2-Undecided

1-Somewhat Disagree

0-Completely Disagree

37) *I enjoy meeting new people and helping them feel welcomed.*

4-Strongly Agree

3-Somewhat Agree

2-Undecided

1-Somewhat Disagree

0-Completely Disagree

38) *I want to serve God with all my time and energy, and am sometimes afraid that marriage or children might get in*

the way.

> 4-Strongly Agree
> 3-Somewhat Agree
> 2-Undecided
> 1-Somewhat Disagree
> 0-Completely Disagree

39) *I often feel like I can understand what a person from another country is saying even though I have never studied their language.*

> 4-Strongly Agree
> 3-Somewhat Agree
> 2-Undecided
> 1-Somewhat Disagree
> 0-Completely Disagree

40) *I am committed to spending large blocks of time on reading and studying Scripture so that I might know biblical truth more fully and accurately.*

> 4-Strongly Agree
> 3-Somewhat Agree
> 2-Undecided
> 1-Somewhat Disagree
> 0-Completely Disagree

41) *I know where groups of people should be headed and the steps they need to take to accomplish the goals of the group.*

> 4-Strongly Agree
> 3-Somewhat Agree
> 2-Undecided
> 1-Somewhat Disagree
> 0-Completely Disagree

42) *I can patiently support those going through painful experiences as they try to stabilize their lives.*

> 4-Strongly Agree
> 3-Somewhat Agree
> 2-Undecided
> 1-Somewhat Disagree
> 0-Completely Disagree

43) *I have often seen God work in desperate life situations by miraculous intervention when I pray.*

> 4-Strongly Agree
> 3-Somewhat Agree
> 2-Undecided
> 1-Somewhat Disagree
> 0-Completely Disagree

44) *I have no desire to own a car, wear nice clothes, buy a house, or go on vacations.*

> 4-Strongly Agree
> 3-Somewhat Agree
> 2-Undecided
> 1-Somewhat Disagree
> 0-Completely Disagree

45) *I have a strong desire to seek out wayward believers and restore them to fellowship with Jesus and the church.*

> 4-Strongly Agree
> 3-Somewhat Agree
> 2-Undecided
> 1-Somewhat Disagree
> 0-Completely Disagree

46) *I often am able to predict the consequences of a particular sinful behavior if a person continues engaging in it.*

> 4-Strongly Agree
> 3-Somewhat Agree
> 2-Undecided
> 1-Somewhat Disagree
> 0-Completely Disagree

47) *I enjoy doing routine tasks to help others.*

4-Strongly Agree

3-Somewhat Agree

2-Undecided

1-Somewhat Disagree

0-Completely Disagree

48) *People often tell me I am able to share difficult truths in ways that are easy to understand.*

4-Strongly Agree

3-Somewhat Agree

2-Undecided

1-Somewhat Disagree

0-Completely Disagree

49) *Sometimes when I do not know what to pray, words come out of my mouth which I do not understand.*

4-Strongly Agree

3-Somewhat Agree

2-Undecided

1-Somewhat Disagree

0-Completely Disagree

50) *I often find simple, practical solutions in the midst of conflict or confusion.*

4-Strongly Agree
3-Somewhat Agree
2-Undecided
1-Somewhat Disagree
0-Completely Disagree

51) *People often look to me for guidance in coordination, organization, and ministry opportunities.*

4-Strongly Agree
3-Somewhat Agree
2-Undecided
1-Somewhat Disagree
0-Completely Disagree

52) *I desire to learn another language, culture, or religion so that I can better connect the truths of the gospel with the people in that culture.*

4-Strongly Agree
3-Somewhat Agree
2-Undecided
1-Somewhat Disagree
0-Completely Disagree

53) *I enjoy making things with my hands.*

4-Strongly Agree

3-Somewhat Agree

2-Undecided

1-Somewhat Disagree

0-Completely Disagree

54) *I have enjoyed being involved in local musical productions or plays.*

4-Strongly Agree

3-Somewhat Agree

2-Undecided

1-Somewhat Disagree

0-Completely Disagree

55) *It is easy for me to tell if a person is honest or dishonest.*

4-Strongly Agree

3-Somewhat Agree

2-Undecided

1-Somewhat Disagree

0-Completely Disagree

56) *I am effective at adapting the gospel message to fit a person's needs or current situation.*

4-Strongly Agree

3-Somewhat Agree

2-Undecided

1-Somewhat Disagree

0-Completely Disagree

57) *I can challenge others without making them feel condemned.*

4-Strongly Agree

3-Somewhat Agree

2-Undecided

1-Somewhat Disagree

0-Completely Disagree

58) *I have unwavering confidence in God's continuing provision to help, even in difficult times.*

4-Strongly Agree

3-Somewhat Agree

2-Undecided

1-Somewhat Disagree

0-Completely Disagree

59) *I like knowing my financial support is making a real difference in the lives of others.*

4-Strongly Agree

3-Somewhat Agree

2-Undecided

1-Somewhat Disagree

0-Completely Disagree

60) *I have prayed for an emotionally ill person and seen the person get better.*

4-Strongly Agree

3-Somewhat Agree

2-Undecided

1-Somewhat Disagree

0-Completely Disagree

61) *I cannot stand idly by while things go undone.*

4-Strongly Agree

3-Somewhat Agree

2-Undecided

1-Somewhat Disagree

0-Completely Disagree

62) *I like to create a place where people do not feel they are alone.*

4-Strongly Agree

3-Somewhat Agree

2-Undecided

1-Somewhat Disagree

0-Completely Disagree

63) *I have never had problems with lust or strong sexual desires.*

> 4-Strongly Agree
> 3-Somewhat Agree
> 2-Undecided
> 1-Somewhat Disagree
> 0-Completely Disagree

64) *It is a strong desire of mine to have all Christians of all languages communicate together.*

> 4-Strongly Agree
> 3-Somewhat Agree
> 2-Undecided
> 1-Somewhat Disagree
> 0-Completely Disagree

65) *I am able to grasp and understand passages in Scripture which others find difficult.*

> 4-Strongly Agree
> 3-Somewhat Agree
> 2-Undecided
> 1-Somewhat Disagree
> 0-Completely Disagree

66) *I am able to influence others to achieve a goal.*

> 4-Strongly Agree
> 3-Somewhat Agree
> 2-Undecided
> 1-Somewhat Disagree
> 0-Completely Disagree

67) *I enjoy helping people sometimes regarded as undeserving or beyond help.*

> 4-Strongly Agree
> 3-Somewhat Agree
> 2-Undecided
> 1-Somewhat Disagree
> 0-Completely Disagree

68) *I believe that if we trusted God more, we would see dramatic, public miracles like in the New Testament.*

> 4-Strongly Agree
> 3-Somewhat Agree
> 2-Undecided
> 1-Somewhat Disagree
> 0-Completely Disagree

69) *I live in communal housing and get my clothes from thrift shops so that I can give more of my income away.*

4-Strongly Agree
3-Somewhat Agree
2-Undecided
1-Somewhat Disagree
0-Completely Disagree

70) *In the past, when helping someone, I try to provide direction for the whole person—relationally, emotionally, spiritually, etc.*

4-Strongly Agree
3-Somewhat Agree
2-Undecided
1-Somewhat Disagree
0-Completely Disagree

71) *I frequently, boldly, and verbally expose cultural trends, teachings, or events to other Christians which contradict biblical principles.*

4-Strongly Agree
3-Somewhat Agree
2-Undecided
1-Somewhat Disagree
0-Completely Disagree

72) *I receive great satisfaction in doing small or trivial*

tasks for others that need to be done.

4-Strongly Agree

3-Somewhat Agree

2-Undecided

1-Somewhat Disagree

0-Completely Disagree

73) *I pay close attention to the words, phrases and meanings of those who teach God's Word.*

4-Strongly Agree

3-Somewhat Agree

2-Undecided

1-Somewhat Disagree

0-Completely Disagree

74) *I frequently speak or pray in a language that I have not learned.*

4-Strongly Agree

3-Somewhat Agree

2-Undecided

1-Somewhat Disagree

0-Completely Disagree

75) *I can anticipate the likely consequence of an individual's or group's action.*

4-Strongly Agree

3-Somewhat Agree

2-Undecided

1-Somewhat Disagree

0-Completely Disagree

76) *The development of effective plans for church ministry or community service gives me great satisfaction.*

4-Strongly Agree

3-Somewhat Agree

2-Undecided

1-Somewhat Disagree

0-Completely Disagree

77) *It is easy for me to move into a new community and make friends.*

4-Strongly Agree

3-Somewhat Agree

2-Undecided

1-Somewhat Disagree

0-Completely Disagree

78) *I am good at and enjoy working with my hands.*

4-Strongly Agree

3-Somewhat Agree

2-Undecided

1-Somewhat Disagree

0-Completely Disagree

79) *If a truth cannot be presented creatively, it would be better to not present it at all.*

4-Strongly Agree

3-Somewhat Agree

2-Undecided

1-Somewhat Disagree

0-Completely Disagree

80) *God has used me to warn others of the danger of a certain teaching.*

4-Strongly Agree

3-Somewhat Agree

2-Undecided

1-Somewhat Disagree

0-Completely Disagree

81) *I openly and confidently tell others what Jesus has done for me, and want others to ask me about my faith.*

4-Strongly Agree

3-Somewhat Agree

2-Undecided

1-Somewhat Disagree

0-Completely Disagree

82) *People express to me how much I've helped or encouraged them in a time of need.*

4-Strongly Agree

3-Somewhat Agree

2-Undecided

1-Somewhat Disagree

0-Completely Disagree

83) *I believe God will help me accomplish great things.*

4-Strongly Agree

3-Somewhat Agree

2-Undecided

1-Somewhat Disagree

0-Completely Disagree

84) *I believe I have been given an abundance of resources so that I may give more to help with the financial needs of others.*

4-Strongly Agree

3-Somewhat Agree

2-Undecided

1-Somewhat Disagree

0-Completely Disagree

85) *When I visit and help those who are sick and pray that God would make them physically whole, they nearly always recover.*

4-Strongly Agree

3-Somewhat Agree

2-Undecided

1-Somewhat Disagree

0-Completely Disagree

86) *The church needs to stop talking so much and start helping people in practical ways.*

4-Strongly Agree

3-Somewhat Agree

2-Undecided

1-Somewhat Disagree

0-Completely Disagree

87) *I make people feel at ease even in unfamiliar surroundings.*

4-Strongly Agree

3-Somewhat Agree

2-Undecided

1-Somewhat Disagree

0-Completely Disagree

88) *When I imagine my future, I rarely envision a spouse or family,*

4-Strongly Agree

3-Somewhat Agree

2-Undecided

1-Somewhat Disagree

0-Completely Disagree

89) *If I hear a Christian speaking in a different language, I find I can understand what they are saying.*

4-Strongly Agree

3-Somewhat Agree

2-Undecided

1-Somewhat Disagree

0-Completely Disagree

90) *I discover important biblical truths when reading or studying Scripture which benefit others in the church.*

4-Strongly Agree

3-Somewhat Agree

2-Undecided

1-Somewhat Disagree

0-Completely Disagree

91) *I can manage people and resources effectively to accomplish set goals.*

    4-Strongly Agree
    3-Somewhat Agree
    2-Undecided
    1-Somewhat Disagree
    0-Completely Disagree

92) *I enjoy doing practical things for people who are in need.*

    4-Strongly Agree
    3-Somewhat Agree
    2-Undecided
    1-Somewhat Disagree
    0-Completely Disagree

93) *I often pray for impossible things which actually come true.*

    4-Strongly Agree
    3-Somewhat Agree
    2-Undecided
    1-Somewhat Disagree
    0-Completely Disagree

94) *I think that materialism, consumerism, capitalism, and greed are some of the greatest problems in the world today.*

> 4-Strongly Agree
> 3-Somewhat Agree
> 2-Undecided
> 1-Somewhat Disagree
> 0-Completely Disagree

95) *I often see other believers respond spiritually to my direction and leadership.*

> 4-Strongly Agree
> 3-Somewhat Agree
> 2-Undecided
> 1-Somewhat Disagree
> 0-Completely Disagree

96) *I am able to understand how key current events around the world tie into Bible prophecy and how these events will affect the future.*

> 4-Strongly Agree
> 3-Somewhat Agree
> 2-Undecided
> 1-Somewhat Disagree

0-Completely Disagree

97) *I often recognize ways that I can care for others indirectly without speaking or teaching.*

> 4-Strongly Agree
> 3-Somewhat Agree
> 2-Undecided
> 1-Somewhat Disagree
> 0-Completely Disagree

98) *I take a systematic approach to my daily study of the Bible.*

> 4-Strongly Agree
> 3-Somewhat Agree
> 2-Undecided
> 1-Somewhat Disagree
> 0-Completely Disagree

99) *God has used me to witness to other people whose language I did not know.*

> 4-Strongly Agree
> 3-Somewhat Agree
> 2-Undecided
> 1-Somewhat Disagree
> 0-Completely Disagree

100) *I have a strong sense of confidence in my solution to problems.*

>4-Strongly Agree
>3-Somewhat Agree
>2-Undecided
>1-Somewhat Disagree
>0-Completely Disagree

101) *I would rather make a decision for a group than persuade them to reach the same decision.*

>4-Strongly Agree
>3-Somewhat Agree
>2-Undecided
>1-Somewhat Disagree
>0-Completely Disagree

102) *The thought of moving to a new community and making new friends is exciting to me.*

>4-Strongly Agree
>3-Somewhat Agree
>2-Undecided
>1-Somewhat Disagree
>0-Completely Disagree

103) *I am able to design and construct things that help others.*

> 4-Strongly Agree
> 3-Somewhat Agree
> 2-Undecided
> 1-Somewhat Disagree
> 0-Completely Disagree

104) *I regularly need to get away from people so that I can reflect and develop my imagination.*

> 4-Strongly Agree
> 3-Somewhat Agree
> 2-Undecided
> 1-Somewhat Disagree
> 0-Completely Disagree

105) *I often have insights into a person's character or motives, and receive confirmation of my perceptions at a later date.*

> 4-Strongly Agree
> 3-Somewhat Agree
> 2-Undecided
> 1-Somewhat Disagree
> 0-Completely Disagree

106) *I seem to be able to determine when a person is prepared to receive Jesus Christ.*

> 4-Strongly Agree
> 3-Somewhat Agree
> 2-Undecided
> 1-Somewhat Disagree
> 0-Completely Disagree

107) *I would rather develop a friendship with a Christian person than a non-Christian.*

> 4-Strongly Agree
> 3-Somewhat Agree
> 2-Undecided
> 1-Somewhat Disagree
> 0-Completely Disagree

108) *I am regularly challenging others to trust God and step out in faith to do difficult things.*

> 4-Strongly Agree
> 3-Somewhat Agree
> 2-Undecided
> 1-Somewhat Disagree
> 0-Completely Disagree

109) *I have great satisfaction in giving large amounts of*

money to others in need.

> 4-Strongly Agree
> 3-Somewhat Agree
> 2-Undecided
> 1-Somewhat Disagree
> 0-Completely Disagree

110) *I feel strongly that my prayers for a sick person bring wholeness to that person.*

> 4-Strongly Agree
> 3-Somewhat Agree
> 2-Undecided
> 1-Somewhat Disagree
> 0-Completely Disagree

111) *I would rather support someone in their ministry than lead a ministry of my own.*

> 4-Strongly Agree
> 3-Somewhat Agree
> 2-Undecided
> 1-Somewhat Disagree
> 0-Completely Disagree

112) *I enjoy cooking meals and preparing my house so that I can share my house with other people.*

4-Strongly Agree

3-Somewhat Agree

2-Undecided

1-Somewhat Disagree

0-Completely Disagree

113) *I am currently single, and am fine with never being married or having children.*

4-Strongly Agree

3-Somewhat Agree

2-Undecided

1-Somewhat Disagree

0-Completely Disagree

114) *When visiting other countries, I find it easy to communicate even though I don't know the language.*

4-Strongly Agree

3-Somewhat Agree

2-Undecided

1-Somewhat Disagree

0-Completely Disagree

115) *It is easy for me to learn difficult truths.*

4-Strongly Agree

3-Somewhat Agree

2-Undecided

1-Somewhat Disagree

0-Completely Disagree

116) *People seem to enjoy following me to do an important task.*

4-Strongly Agree

3-Somewhat Agree

2-Undecided

1-Somewhat Disagree

0-Completely Disagree

117) *I enjoy ministering to a person who is sick in the hospital.*

4-Strongly Agree

3-Somewhat Agree

2-Undecided

1-Somewhat Disagree

0-Completely Disagree

118) *God often provides answers to my prayers with unordinary means.*

4-Strongly Agree

3-Somewhat Agree

2-Undecided
1-Somewhat Disagree
0-Completely Disagree

119) *If I die with more than $1000 to my name, I will consider my ministry a failure.*

4-Strongly Agree
3-Somewhat Agree
2-Undecided
1-Somewhat Disagree
0-Completely Disagree

120) *Other Christians frequently come to me with their cares and spiritual worries.*

4-Strongly Agree
3-Somewhat Agree
2-Undecided
1-Somewhat Disagree
0-Completely Disagree

121) *I often speak the truth, even in places where it is unpopular or difficult for people to accept.*

4-Strongly Agree
3-Somewhat Agree
2-Undecided

1-Somewhat Disagree

0-Completely Disagree

122) *I don't mind helping others even if they are undeserving or take advantage of me.*

4-Strongly Agree

3-Somewhat Agree

2-Undecided

1-Somewhat Disagree

0-Completely Disagree

123) *I am always looking for better ways to explain things to people so they can grow spiritually and personally.*

4-Strongly Agree

3-Somewhat Agree

2-Undecided

1-Somewhat Disagree

0-Completely Disagree

124) *I find it easy to quickly learn foreign languages.*

4-Strongly Agree

3-Somewhat Agree

2-Undecided

1-Somewhat Disagree

0-Completely Disagree

125) *When people follow my advice in difficult situations, things often turn out well.*

> 4-Strongly Agree
> 3-Somewhat Agree
> 2-Undecided
> 1-Somewhat Disagree
> 0-Completely Disagree

GIFT PROFILE ANSWER SHEET

1	Administration	1	26	51	76	101	=
2	Apostleship (Missionary)	2	27	52	77	102	=
3	Craftsmanship	3	28	53	78	103	=
4	Creative Communication	4	29	54	79	104	=
5	Discernment	5	30	55	80	105	=
6	Evangelism	6	31	56	81	106	=
7	Exhortation or Encouragement	7	32	57	82	107	=
8	Faith	8	33	58	83	108	=
9	Giving	9	34	59	84	109	=
10	Healing	10	35	60	85	110	=
11	Helping	11	36	61	86	111	=
12	Hospitality	12	37	62	87	112	=

13	Celibacy	13	38	63	88	113	=
14	Interpretation	14	39	64	89	114	=
15	Knowledge	15	40	65	90	115	=
16	Leadership	16	41	66	91	116	=
17	Mercy or Compassion	17	42	67	92	117	=
18	Miracles	18	43	68	93	118	=
19	Voluntary Poverty	19	44	69	94	119	=
20	Pastor-Teacher	20	45	70	95	120	=
21	Prophecy	21	46	71	96	121	=
22	Service	22	47	72	97	122	=
23	Teaching	23	48	73	98	123	=
24	Tongues	24	49	74	99	124	=
25	Wisdom	25	50	75	100	125	=

PLEASE NOTE:

This test is not infallible.

Confirmation comes only through repeated cycles of practice
and reassessment.

DOMINANT GIFTS

_____

_____

_____

_____

_____

_____

_____

ABOUT JEREMY MYERS

Jeremy Myers is an author, blogger, podcaster, and Bible teacher who lives in Oregon with his wife and three daughters. He primarily writes at RedeemingGod.com, where he seeks to help liberate people from the shackles of religion. His site also provides an online discipleship group where thousands of like-minded people discuss life and theology and encourage each other to follow Jesus into the world.

If you appreciated the content of this book, would you consider recommending it to your friends and leaving a review on Amazon, iTunes, or Kobo? Thanks!

JOIN JEREMY MYERS AND LEARN MORE

Take Bible and theology courses by joining Jeremy at
RedeemingGod.com/join/

Receive updates about free books, discounted books, and new books by joining Jeremy at
RedeemingGod.com/read-books/

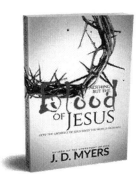

NOTHING BUT THE BLOOD OF JESUS: HOW THE SACRIFICE OF JESUS SAVES THE WORLD FROM SIN

Do you have difficulties reconciling God's behavior in the Old Testament with that of Jesus in the New?

Do you find yourself trying to rationalize God's violent demeanor in the Bible to unbelievers or even to yourself?

Does it seem disconcerting that God tells us not to kill others but He then takes part in some of the bloodiest wars and vindictive genocides in history?

The answer to all such questions is found in Jesus on the cross. By focusing your eyes on Jesus Christ and Him crucified, you come to understand that God was never angry at human sinners, and that no blood sacrifice was ever needed to purchase God's love, forgiveness, grace, and mercy.

In *Nothing but the Blood of Jesus*, J. D. Myers shows how the death of Jesus on the cross reveals the truth about the five concepts of sin, law, sacrifice, scapegoating, and bloodshed. After carefully defining each, this book shows how these definitions provide clarity on numerous biblical texts.

REVIEWS

Building on his previous book, "The Atonement of God," the work of René Girard and a solid grounding in the Scriptures, Jeremy Myers shares fresh and challenging insights with us about sin, law, sacrifice, scapegoating and blood. This book reveals to us how truly precious the blood of Jesus is and the way of escaping the cycle of blame, rivalry, scapegoating, sacrifice and violence that has plagued humanity since the time of Cain and Abel. "Nothing but the Blood of Jesus" is an important and timely literary contribution to a world desperately in need of the non-violent message of Jesus. —Wesley Rostoll

My heart was so filled with joy while reading this book. Jeremy you've reminded me once more that as you walk with Jesus and spend time in His presence, He talks to you and reveals Himself through the Scriptures. —Reader

Purchase the Book Online

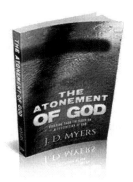

THE ATONEMENT OF GOD: BUILDING YOUR THEOLOGY ON A CRUCIVISION OF GOD

After reading this book, you will never read the Bible the same way again.

By reading this book, you will learn to see God in a whole new light. You will also learn to see yourself in a whole new light, and learn to live life in a whole new way.

The book begins with a short explanation of the various views of the atonement, including an explanation and defense of the "Non-Violent View" of the atonement. This view argues that God did not need or demand the death of Jesus in order to forgive sins. In fact, God has never been angry with us at all, but has always loved and always forgiven.

Following this explanation of the atonement, J. D. Myers takes you on a journey through 10 areas of theology which are radically changed and transformed by the Non-Violent view of the atonement. Read this book, and let your life and theology look more and more like Jesus Christ!

REVIEWS

Outstanding book! Thank you for helping me understand "Crucivision" and the "Non-Violent Atonement." Together, they help it all make sense and fit so well into my personal thinking about God. I am encouraged to be truly free to love and forgive, because God has always loved and forgiven without condition, because Christ exemplified this grace on the Cross, and because the Holy Spirit is in the midst of all life, continuing to show the way through people like you. –Samuel R. Mayer

This book gives another view of the doctrines we have been taught all of our lives. And this actually makes more sense than what we have heard. I myself have had some of these thoughts but couldn't quite make the sense of it all by myself. J.D. Myers helped me answer some questions and settle some confusion for my doctrinal views. This is truly a refreshing read. Jesus really is the demonstration of who God is and God is much easier to understand than being so mean and vindictive in the Old Testament. The tension between the wrath of God and His justice and the love of God are eased when reading this understanding of the atonement. Read with an open mind and enjoy! –Clare N. Bez

Purchase the Book Online

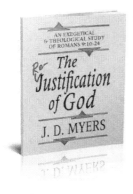

THE RE-JUSTIFICATION OF GOD: A STUDY OF ROMANS 9:10-24

Romans 9 has been a theological battleground for centuries. Scholars from all perspectives have debated whether Paul is teaching corporate or individual election, whether or not God truly hates Esau, and how to understand the hardening of Pharaoh's heart. Both sides have accused the other of misrepresenting God.

In this book, J. D. Myers presents a mediating position. Gleaning from both Calvinistic and Arminian insights into Romans 9, J. D. Myers presents a beautiful portrait of God as described by the pen of the Apostle Paul.

Here is a way to read Romans 9 which allows God to remain sovereign and free, but also allows our theology to avoid the deterministic tendencies which have entrapped certain systems of the past.

Read this book and—maybe for the first time—learn to see God the way Paul saw Him.

REVIEWS

Fantastic read! Jeremy Myers has a gift for seeing things from outside of the box and making it easy to understand for the rest of us. The Re -Justification of God provides a fresh and insightful look into Romans 9:10-24 by interpreting it within the context of chapters 9-11 and then fitting it into the framework of Paul's entire epistle as well. Jeremy manages to provide a solid theological exegesis on a widely misunderstood portion of scripture without it sounding to academic. Most importantly, it provides us with a better view and understanding of who God is. If I had a list of ten books that I thought every Christian should read, this one would be on the list. – Wesley Rostoll

I loved this book! It made me cry and fall in love with God all over again. Romans is one of my favorite books, but now my eyes have been opened to what Paul was really saying. I knew in my heart that God was the good guy, but J. D. Myers provided the analysis to prove the text. … I can with great confidence read the difficult chapters of Romans, and my furrowed brow is eased. Thank you, J. D. Myers. I love God, even more and am so grateful that his is so longsuffering in his perfect love! Well done. –Treinhart

Purchase the Book Online

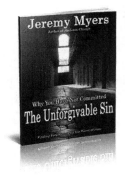

WHY YOU HAVE NOT COMMITTED THE UNFORGIVABLE SIN: FINDING FORGIVENESS FOR THE WORST OF SINS

Are you afraid that you have committed the unforgivable sin?

In this book, you will learn what this sin is and why you have not committed it. After surveying the various views about blasphemy against the Holy Spirit and examining Matthew 12:31-32, you will learn what the sin is and how it is committed.

As a result of reading this book, you will gain freedom from the fear of committing the worst of all sins, and learn how much God loves you!

REVIEWS

This book addressed things I have struggled and felt pandered to for years, and helped to bring wholeness to my heart again. –Natalie Fleming

A great read, on a controversial subject; biblical, historical and contextually treated to give the greatest understanding. May be the best on this subject (and there is very few) ever written. – Tony Vance

You must read this book. Forgiveness is necessary to see your blessings. So if you purchase this book, [you will have] no regrets. —Virtuous Woman

Jeremy Myers covers this most difficult topic thoroughly and with great compassion. —J. Holland

Wonderful explication of the unpardonable sin. God loves you more than you know. May Jesus Christ be with you always. —Robert M Sawin III

Excellent book! Highly recommend for anyone who has anxiety and fear about having committed the unforgivable sin. —William Tom

As someone who is constantly worried that they have disappointed or offended God, this book was, quite literally, a "Godsend." I thought I had committed this sin as I swore against the Holy Spirit in my mind. It only started after reading the verse about it in the Bible. The swear words against Him came into my mind over and over and I couldn't seem to stop no matter how much I prayed. I was convinced I was going to hell and cried constantly. I was extremely worried and depressed. This book has allowed me to breathe again, to have hope again. Thank you, Jeremy. I will read and re-read. I believe this book was definitely God inspired. I only wish I had found it sooner. —Sue

Purchase the Book Online

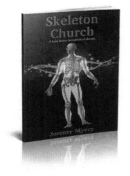

SKELETON CHURCH: A BARE-BONES DEFINITION OF CHURCH (PREFACE TO THE CLOSE YOUR CHURCH FOR GOOD BOOK SERIES)

The church has a skeleton which is identical in all types of churches. Unity and peace can develop in Christianity if we recognize this skeleton as the simple, bare-bones definition of church. But when we focus on the outer trappings—the skin, hair, and eye color, the clothes, the muscle tone, and other outward appearances—division and strife form within the church.

Let us return to the skeleton church and grow in unity once again.

REVIEWS

I worried about buying another book that aimed at reducing things to a simple minimum, but the associations of the author along with the price gave me reason to hope and means to see. I really liked this book. First, because it wasn't identical to what other simple church people are saying. He adds unique elements that are worth reading. Second, the size is small enough to read, think, and pray about without getting lost. –Abel Barba

In *Skeleton Church*, Jeremy Myers makes us rethink church. For Myers, the church isn't a style of worship, a row of pews, or even a building. Instead, the church is the people of God, which provides the basic skeletal structure of the church. The muscles, parts, and flesh of the church are how we carry Jesus' mission into our own neighborhoods in our own unique ways. This eBook will make you see the church differently. –Travis Mamone

This book gets back to the basics of the New Testament church—who we are as Christians and what our perspective should be in the world we live in today. Jeremy cuts away all the institutional layers of a church and gets to the heart of our purpose as Christians in the world we live in and how to affect the people around us with God heart and view in mind. Not a physical church in mind. It was a great book and I have read it twice now. – Vaughn Bender

The Skeleton Church ... Oh. My. Word. Why aren't more people reading this!? It was well-written, explained everything beautifully, and it was one of the best explanations of how God intended for church to be. Not to mention an easy read! The author took it all apart, the church, and showed us how it should be. He made it real. If you are searching to find something or someone to show you what God intended for the church, this is the book you need to read. –Ericka

Purchase the Book Online

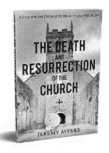

THE DEATH AND RESUR-RECTION OF THE CHURCH (VOLUME 1 IN THE CLOSE YOUR CHURCH FOR GOOD BOOK SERIES)

In a day when many are looking for ways to revital-ize the church, Jeremy Myers argues that the church should die ... so that it can rise again.

This is not only because of the universal principle that death precedes resurrection, but also because the church has adopted certain Satanic values and goals and the only way to break free from our enslavement to these values is to die.

But death will not be the end of the church, just as death was not the end of Jesus. If the church follows Jesus into death, and even to the hellish places on earth, it is only then that the church will rise again to new life and vibrancy in the Kingdom of God.

REVIEWS

I have often thought on the church and how its ac-ceptance of corporate methods and assimilation of cul-tural media mores taints its mission but Jeremy Myers el-oquently captures in words the true crux of the matter—

that the church is not a social club for do-gooders but to disseminate the good news to all the nooks and crannies in the world and particularly and primarily those bastions in the reign of evil. That the "gates of Hell" Jesus pronounces indicate that the church is in an offensive, not defensive, posture as gates are defensive structures.

I must confess that in reading I was inclined to be in agreement as many of the same thinkers that Myers riffs upon have influenced me also—Walter Wink, Robert Farrar Capon, Greg Boyd, NT Wright, etc. So as I read, I frequently nodded my head in agreement. –GN Trifanaff

The book is well written, easy to understand, organized and consistent thoughts. It rightfully makes the reader at least think about things as … is "the way we have always done it" necessarily the Biblical or Christ-like way, or is it in fact very sinful?! I would recommend the book for pastors and church officers; those who have the most moving-and-shaking clout to implement changes, or keep things the same. –Joel M. Wilson

Absolutely phenomenal. Unless we let go of everything Adamic in our nature, we cannot embrace anything Christlike. For the church to die, we the individual temples must dig our graves. It is a must read for all who take issues about the body of Christ seriously. –Mordecai Petersburg

Purchase the Book Online

PUT SERVICE BACK INTO THE CHURCH SERVICE (VOLUME 2 IN THE CLOSE YOUR CHURCH FOR GOOD BOOK SERIES)

Churches around the world are trying to revitalize their church services. There is almost nothing they will not try. Some embark on multi-million dollar building campaigns while others sell their buildings to plant home churches. Some hire celebrity pastors to attract crowds of people, while others hire no clergy so that there can be open sharing in the service.

Yet despite everything churches have tried, few focus much time, money, or energy on the one thing that churches are supposed to be doing: loving and serving others like Jesus.

Put Service Back into the Church Service challenges readers to follow a few simple principles and put a few ideas into practice which will help churches of all types and sizes make serving others the primary emphasis of a church service.

REVIEWS

Jeremy challenges church addicts, those addicted to an unending parade of church buildings, church services, Bible studies, church programs and more to follow Jesus into our communities, communities filled with lonely, hurting people and BE the church, loving the people in our world with the love of Jesus. Do we need another training program, another seminar, another church building, a remodeled church building, more staff, updated music, or does our world need us, the followers of Jesus, to BE the church in the world? The book is well-written, challenging and a book that really can make a difference not only in our churches, but also and especially in our neighborhoods and communities. –Charles Epworth

I just finished *Put Service Back Into Church Service* by Jeremy Myers, and as with his others books I have read on the church, it was very challenging. For those who love Jesus, but are questioning the function of the traditional brick and mortar church, and their role in it, this is a must read. It may be a bit unsettling to the reader who is still entrenched in traditional "church," but it will make you think, and possibly re-evaluate your role in the church. Get this book, and all others on the church by Jeremy. –Ward Kelly

Purchase the Book Online

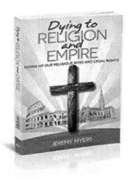

DYING TO RELIGION AND EMPIRE (VOLUME 3 IN THE CLOSE YOUR CHURCH FOR GOOD BOOK SERIES)

Could Christianity exist without religious rites or legal rights? In *Dying to Religion and Empire*, I not only answer this question with an emphatic "Yes!" but argue that if the church is going to thrive in the coming decades, we must give up our religious rites and legal rights.

Regarding religious rites, I call upon the church to abandon the quasi-magical traditions of water baptism and the Lord's Supper and transform or redeem these practices so that they reflect the symbolic meaning and intent which they had in New Testament times.

Furthermore, the church has become far too dependent upon certain legal rights for our continued existence. Ideas such as the right to life, liberty, and the pursuit of happiness are not conducive to living as the people of God who are called to follow Jesus into servanthood and death. Also, reliance upon the freedom of speech, the freedom of assembly, and other such freedoms as established by the Bill of Rights have made the church a servant of the state rather than a servant of God and the gospel. Such freedoms must be forsaken if we are going to live within the rule and reign of God on earth.

This book not only challenges religious and political liberals but conservatives as well. It is a call to leave behind the comfortable religion we know, and follow Jesus into the uncertain and wild ways of radical discipleship. To rise and live in the reality of God's Kingdom, we must first die to religion and empire.

REVIEWS

Jeremy is one of the freshest, freest authors out there—and you need to hear what he has to say. This book is startling and new in thought and conclusion. Are the "sacraments" inviolate? Why? Do you worship at a secular altar? Conservative? Liberal? Be prepared to open your eyes. Mr. Myers will not let you keep sleeping!

Jeremy Myers is one or the most thought provoking authors that I read, this book has really helped me to look outside the box and start thinking how can I make more sense of my relationship with Christ and how can I show others in a way that impacts them the way that Jesus' disciples impacted their world. Great book, great author. – Brett Hotchkiss

Purchase the eBook

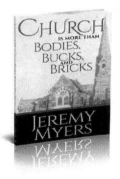

CHURCH IS MORE THAN BODIES, BUCKS, & BRICKS (VOLUME 4 IN THE CLOSE YOUR CHURCH FOR GOOD BOOK SERIES)

Many people define church as a place and time where people gather, a way for ministry money to be given and spent, and a building in which people regularly meet on Sunday mornings.

In this book, author and blogger Jeremy Myers shows that church is more than bodies, bucks, and bricks.

Church is the people of God who follow Jesus into the world, and we can be the church no matter how many people we are with, no matter the size of our church budget, and regardless of whether we have a church building or not.

By abandoning our emphasis on more people, bigger budgets, and newer buildings, we may actually liberate the church to better follow Jesus into the world.

REVIEWS

This book does more than just identify issues that have been bothering me about church as we know it, but it goes into history and explains how we got here. In this way it is similar to Viola's *Pagan Christianity*, but I found it a much more enjoyable read. Jeremy goes into more detail on the three issues he covers as well as giving a lot of practical advice on how to remedy these situations. – Portent

Since I returned from Africa 20 years ago I have struggled with going to church back in the States. This book helped me not feel guilty and has helped me process this struggle. It is challenging and overflows with practical suggestions. He loves the church despite its imperfections and suggests ways to break the bondage we find ourselves in. –Truealian

Jeremy Meyers always writes a challenging book ... It seems the American church (as a whole) is very comfortable with the way things are ... The challenge is to get out of the brick and mortar buildings and stagnant programs and minister to the needy in person with funds in hand to meet their needs especially to the widows and orphans as we are directed in the scriptures. –GGTexas

Purchase the Book Online

CRUCIFORM PASTORAL LEADERSHIP (VOLUME 5 IN THE CLOSE YOUR CHURCH FOR GOOD BOOK SERIES)

This book is forthcoming in early 2019.

The final volume in the *Close Your Church for Good* book series look at issues related to pastoral leadership in the church. It discusses topics such as preaching and pastoral pay from the perspective of the cross.

The best way pastors can lead their church is by following Jesus to the cross!

This book will be published in early 2019.

ADVENTURES IN FISHING (FOR MEN)

Adventures in Fishing (for Men) is a satirical look at evangelism and church growth strategies.

Using fictional accounts from his attempts to become a world-famous fisherman, Jeremy Myers shows how many of the evangelism and church growth strategies of today do little to actually reach the world for Jesus Christ.

Adventures in Fishing (for Men) pokes fun at some of the popular evangelistic techniques and strategies endorsed and practiced by many Christians in today's churches. The stories in this book show in humorous detail how little we understand the culture that surrounds us or how to properly reach people with the gospel of Jesus Christ. The story also shows how much time, energy, and money goes into evangelism preparation and training with the end result being that churches rarely accomplish any actual evangelism.

REVIEWS

I found *Adventures in Fishing (For Men)* quite funny! Jeremy Myers does a great job shining the light on some of the more common practices in Evangelism today. His allegory gently points to the foolishness that is found within a system that takes the preaching of the gospel and tries to reduce it to a simplified formula. A formula that takes what should be an organic, Spirit led experience and turns it into a gospel that is nutritionally benign.

If you have ever EE'd someone you may find Myers' book offensive, but if you have come to the place where you realize that Evangelism isn't a matter of a script and checklists, then you might benefit from this light-hearted peek at Evangelism today. –Jennifer L. Davis

Adventures in Fishing (for Men) is good book in understanding evangelism to be more than just being a set of methods or to do list to follow. –Ashok Daniel

Purchase the Book Online

CHRISTMAS REDEMPTION: WHY CHRISTIANS SHOULD CELEBRATE A PAGAN HOLIDAY

Christmas Redemption looks at some of the symbolism and traditions of Christmas, including gifts, the Christmas tree, and even Santa Claus and shows how all of these can be celebrated and enjoyed by Christians as a true and accurate reflection of the gospel.

Though Christmas used to be a pagan holiday, it has been redeemed by Jesus.

If you have been told that Christmas is a pagan holiday and is based on the Roman festival of Saturnalia, or if you have been told that putting up a Christmas tree is idolatrous, or if you have been told that Santa Claus is Satanic and teaches children to be greedy, then you must read this book! In it, you will learn that all of these Christmas traditions have been redeemed by Jesus and are good and healthy ways of celebrating the truth of the gospel and the grace of Jesus Christ.

REVIEWS

Too many times we as Christians want to condemn nearly everything around us and in so doing become much like the Pharisees and religious leaders that Jesus encountered. I recommend this book to everyone who has concerns of how and why we celebrate Christmas. I recommend it to those who do not have any qualms in celebrating but may not know the history of Christmas. I recommend this book to everyone, no matter who or where you are, no matter your background or beliefs, no matter whether you are young or old. —David H.

Very informative book dealing with the roots of our modern Christmas traditions. The Biblical teaching on redemption is excellent! Highly recommended. —Tamara

This is a wonderful book full of hope and joy. The book explains where Christmas traditions originated and how they have been changed and been adapted over the years. The hope that the grace that is hidden in the celebrations will turn more hearts to the Lord's call is very evident. Jeremy Myers has given us a lovely gift this Christmas. His insights will lift our hearts and remain with us a long time. —Janet Cardoza

I love how the author uses multiple sources to back up his opinions. He doesn't just use bible verses, he goes back into the history of the topics (pagan rituals, Santa, etc.) as well. Great book! —Jenna G.

Purchase the Book Online

JOIN JEREMY MYERS AND LEARN MORE

Take Bible and theology courses by joining Jeremy at
RedeemingGod.com/join/

Receive updates about free books, discounted books,
and new books by joining Jeremy at
RedeemingGod.com/read-books/

56545452R00100

Made in the USA
Columbia, SC
27 April 2019